Psycho-Sales-Analysis

Sharpen your selling skills with

The New Art of

Psycho-Sales-Analysis

by Jack Huttig

Self-Taught Sales Success

1978

LITTLEFIELD, ADAMS & CO.
TOTOWA, NEW JERSEY

Reprinted 1973, 1978
by
Littlefield, Adams & Co.
by arrangement with
Nelson-Hall Co., Publishers

Library of Congress Catalog Card No. 72-95367

Printed in the United States of America

To Middy

The kind of wife
every salesman should have.

About the Author

Jack Huttig is manager of the marketing manpower development division for Beech Aircraft Corporation of Wichita, Kansas. His major responsibilities include the development and implementation of recruiting, testing, evaluating and training of salesmen, sales managers and other marketing personnel. Also, he conducts fields sales training programs, seminars and workshops, and administers cooperative educational programs in conjunction with leading American universities.

A graduate of Wichita State University, Mr. Huttig began his business career as a salesman. Working for different companies, he advanced to sales manager, public relations administrator, advertising manager and sales promotion manager.

His writing and promotional activities have been recognized with awards, especially from the Freedoms Foundation of Valley Forge, Kansas City Sales and Marketing Executives Club, and *Writer's Digest*.

About the Book

Jack Huttig, internationally-known for his proficiency in training salesmen, helps you master the principles of professional selling much as he does in his famous workshops. Brushing aside pep talks and clichés, he presents an imaginative but practical program which encourages you to teach yourself the art of successful selling.

Everything you need to know about professional selling is explained. The author offers a fresh and revealing approach to familiar problems such as finding prospects, developing markets, sparking interest, overcoming objections, using sales aids, and closing sales (7 ways).

This book will increase your selling power and income no matter what you sell, where you live, or what your social and educational background. Basic selling fundamentals never change, even though people, customs and products or services may. The objective is to learn them and use them in your everyday selling effort. Because the theory is flexible, it allows you to select only those techniques which fit your individual sales program.

Step by step, as you climb what Mr. Huttig calls "the Golden Stairway to Successful Sales," you learn how to plan, organize, utilize your time, and put into effect, through educated effort, your personal selling method. He proves that salesmanship, scientifically used, can offer just as much security, growth, and often as much income and prestige as law, medicine and engineering.

Contents

Illustrations

Preface

Never before have so many said
so much to benefit so few.

Each time I suffer through a long dissertation on sales-manship or leaf through page after page of inspirational sales clichés, this paraphrased remark comes to mind. It was voiced many years ago by a fellow salesman as we walked, disillusioned, from the last boring session of a week-long seminar. Those who have squirmed in their seats at sales schools or grown tired-eyed attempting to distill a few simple facts from pedantic volumes will share my concern for the plight of others forced to undergo similar training.

I have, therefore, attempted to organize and report the basics of selling in a compact workbook form which can be easily read, quickly understood, and profitably used by salesmen in their daily business life. This book is the result.

No apology is offered for the condensation of thought since brevity will surely be a welcomed change for any student of marketing subjects.

Should this effort stir your imagination and help you develop the planned and organized selling patterns of the successful sales professional, then it will have served its intended purpose.

Jack Huttig

Acknowledgments

Anyone attempting to write a book will sooner or later recognize that its contents can never be solely and exclusively the writer's own thoughts and opinions. In any work he attempts there will be thoughts gleaned from other books, ideas supplied by other people, opinions shaped by contemporaries, and facts known first to associates. I, for example, have never met a man who did not possess some knowledge, some thought or idea, or some distinctive mental or physical capability which I lacked.

Those who have supplied the employment in which the writer's trade was learned, those who have counseled and advised as professionals and friends, and those who have shared their knowledge with the writer are deserving of acknowledgement.

It would be impossible, of course, to list all the people who have influenced the contents of this book. But some, because of their more immediate assistance, merit this writer's most sincere "thank you." These people are:

O. A. Beech	Frank E. Hedrick
Wyman L. Henry	Austin Rising
Leddy Greever	M. G. Neuburger
John J. Funsch	Walter Gunstream
H. A. Anderson	D. C. Hornberger
R. E. Mallonee	Eldon M. Bloyd
W. F. Balzerick	W. D. Gremp
John Pike	W. G. West
Paul McGarrah	Larry A. Ball
Karl H. Berg	V. L. Gaston

Robert Buettgenbach	Rex Lorence
Alan K. Wharry	Jerry Warner
M. P. Eaton	R. J. Yarnell
George Humphry	H. S. Gregory
Marion Stevens	L. F. Sander
R. G. Coker	Paul Dannelley

and the many professional salesmen it has been my pleasure and privilege to know.

Section 1

The not-so-secret road to self-taught sales success

Take a moment and think about the highly successful salesmen you've known in your lifetime. You'll quickly recognize that these successful men are different individuals with different sociological backgrounds, different educations, and different mental capabilities. They sell different products to different customers in different businesses in different localities. In fact, the only common denominator shared by these successful salesmen appears to be *"uncommonness."*

But think a little longer and a little harder and you'll come to a very important conclusion. Although each of these successful salesmen is different in countless ways, every one of these men followed exactly the same road to sales success. They first learned selling fundamentals, and then they learned how to apply those selling fundamentals in their day-by-day sales activities.

Twenty-five years spent in selling everything from road oil to roof coatings and advertising to airplanes has convinced me that *unsuccessful* salesmen fall into two general categories:

- Salesmen who *don't know* basic selling principles.
- Salesmen who *can't apply* the basic selling principles they have learned.

It's only fair to point out that learning the basic fundamentals of selling is not an easy task. The problem is not the lack of available information but the fact that too much information is available.

Look on the shelf of any respectably sized library or bookstore and you'll find a wide and varied assortment of salesmanship books designed to serve the needs of America's knowledge-hungry salesmen. Almost every conceivable subject from clinical sales psychology to high-pressure closing tactics is thoroughly covered. Thick books, thin books, scholarly texts, or inspirational "sizzle" books — take your choice. Like the shipwrecked sailor with "water, water everywhere but not a drop to drink," today's salesman is surrounded by books that inspire, cajole, and supposedly motivate while offering cliched solutions to generalized problems. Very few of these books clearly define the fundamentals of selling. The few books which do present selling basics in understandable form are seldom able to help the salesman make practical use of this information. Reading and learning is one thing, making practical use of the knowledge is quite another.

Selling fundamentals do not change

It should be mentioned that selling fundamentals have changed little in all the countless centuries man has been selling to his fellow man. As a professional sales trainer, I have attempted to keep abreast of the major published efforts in marketing to search for new ideas which might be used to update and modernize sales-training concepts. As of this writing the search has been fruitless. In the hundreds of books and magazines reviewed, only one significant fact has consistently emerged: *basic sales principles do not change.*

Despite all claims to the contrary, the simple truth is this: There are no magic formulas which can "double your sales in 30 days." There are, however, basic sales principles which have been known and used by successful salesmen for thousands of years. And these basic sales principles, when properly applied, are so effective that they may appear to be magic, at least in the eyes of those who have not yet learned them or do not know how to apply them.

The birth of Psycho-Sales-Analysis

While conducting sales seminars and workshops throughout the United States and Canada, I searched constantly for new and better ways to help salesmen understand and use basic selling techniques. Most of the salesmen I talked with already knew basic selling principles. But the fact remained that they either would not or could not make use of the knowledge they had gained.

These salesmen were much like the farmer who refused to attend the state agricultural college "because," he said, "I'm not farming now half as good as I already know how to." So the problem became one of finding the proper instructional technique to help salesmen help themselves.

As soon as the problem had been properly isolated and defined, the solution was relatively simple. "Ask the salesmen to compare the known with the unknown," an educator-friend suggested. "Ask them to outline their present selling methods and techniques, compare these methods and techniques with basic sales principles *as they are being reviewed,* and then outline corrective action."

What we were now saying to the salesmen in our seminar sessions was something like this:

- You tell us how you're selling now.
- We'll tell you how other salesmen have sold successfully for many, many years.
- Then you decide which of the basic sales techniques will best fit into your own personal selling program and help you increase your sales.

The results of the first experimental workshops to use this instructional technique were both exciting and rewarding. Salesmen who previously experienced great difficulty in relating lecture material to their own sales problems were now able to grasp both the basic principles and their practical application.

Now, at last, the salesmen could see the true value of basic selling techniques. Now they could plan and organize their own personal sales programs while the review of basics was still fresh in their minds.

Surprisingly, the experience level of the salesmen made little difference in their ability to benefit from this program. A Michigan airplane dealer, in business for more than 10 years, attended a refresher sales training course because his sales were lagging. He returned home and sold 8 airplanes within 30 days. (His previous sales record had been 3 airplanes in one month.)

A young Texas machinery salesman with only a few months' experience became his company's leading salesman in the first year following exposure to this known-to-unknown sales training technique.

A name is coined

The success of this training procedure was repeated in workshop after workshop, and a definitive name was coined to describe this combination of educational and selling concepts. To develop his latent sales power, the salesman was asked to use his mental processes (*psycho*) to compare his present selling methods with selling fundamentals (*sales-analysis*). The term Psycho-Sales-Analysis was born!

Psycho-Sales-Analysis was now a tested and proven procedure for professionally conducted seminars and workshops. But what about the hundreds of thousands of salesmen who could not attend these training sessions? Would a self-study book employing this procedure of known-to-unknown comparison help them analyze their sales problems and become more successful? Specifically, would such a self-study book be of help to the salesman who was already successful, and enable him to reach a higher plateau of sales success?

An authority gives his opinion

To find an answer to these questions, a preliminary draft of this book was sent to a number of highly successful salesmen, including Robert L. Shackelford.

Bob Shackelford began his sales career at the end of World War II as a war surplus materials salesman. He sold surplus machinery and climbed the sales ladder to ownership of a large construction company. Would a comparative review of basic sales techniques be of value to him? His return letter contained this paragraph:

"I read every word. The whole sequence had an objective honesty that was irresistible reading. I'll confess that I started to skim the material but ended up by reading every word. I plan to read it again and again."

Remember, here is a man who started his career by selling used machinery and now owns his own company. He is still intrigued with the basic selling techniques which enabled him to achieve his success. His letter continued:

"What is wrong with an era where more do not and will not take advantage of such valuable guidelines? What's happened to the joy of accomplishment, the pride of self-improvement and self-respect, to say nothing about the desire for security? *If the average salesman would just follow these basic precepts, step by step, he would be devastatingly effective.* But where is the motivation today?"

It is my personal belief that the motivation does exist today. It exists in inexperienced salesmen who have an insatiable appetite for knowledge and the driving desire to succeed. And it exists in experienced salesmen who are willing to reopen their minds, to study, and to use again the basic sales principles they once knew.

Thus another sales book is being added to America's overcrowded bookshelves. This book offers no shortcut to success, no promise of magic formulas; but it does offer proven principles and techniques which can make *you* as successful as they have made thousands of other "Mr. Shackelfords."

My intent is to show you (if you don't already know) or to remind you (if you've forgotten) how to think, organize, and sell as a professional.

I claim no originality or inspired thought regarding the principles and techniques discussed in this book. These selling fundamentals were borrowed from the millions of professional salesmen who, through the centuries, have been more successful than their contemporaries simply because they took the time to learn *and apply* the basic selling techniques used by other successful salesmen before them.

I ask only that you follow the proven Psycho-Sales-Analysis procedure of writing down answers to the questions about your present sales methods before you read each section. Then, after reading each section, that you write down the ways in which you can profitably use the basic sales techniques you've learned.

Thinking and writing result in learning

Why do all this writing? There's a very simple reason. If you write down your answer you'll be forced to think. Thinking and writing reinforce the learning process. Since you are the one who is to benefit, you are the one who will have to do the thinking and the writing.

There's a reward for your efforts, of course. If you follow this proven procedure I can guarantee that the latent sales power now dormant within you will flower into full bloom.

As you'll soon see, there's really nothing complicated

about the requirements for success in the sales profession. All it takes is planning, organization, and educated effort — *your effort.*

So let's take pencil in hand and answer the profitable challenge that lies in the pages ahead.

The measure of a man's success in business is his ability to organize.

— *Elbert Hubbard*

Section 2

Psycho-Sales-Analysis Guide

*Before reading Section 2, write
your answers to these questions:*

1. Why did I decide to become a salesman?

2. What do I like best about my job?

3. What do I like least about my job?

4. Which of my friends and neighbors have "better jobs"?

5. Why do I feel their jobs are better than mine?

6. How does my wife feel about my work as a salesman?

7. Would I want my son to be a salesman?

8. Why did I answer question 7 this way?

9. In what ways does my job help:
    a. My family?
    b. My community?
    c. My customers?

The rebirth of a salesman

SALESMEN, I firmly believe, are among the most fortunate people in the world. No other profession allows a man to get up in the morning with yesterday's mistakes so unimportant and the future so unlimited. Accountants, lawyers, doctors, and other professional people are judged on their past performance. The things they did yesterday largely determine the things they can accomplish today.

A salesman, on the other hand, can be a complete failure one day and a success the next merely by capitalizing on the opportunities the new day presents. The salesman, alone among the professionals, has the chance to start fresh each and every day. He has the golden opportunity to progress as far as his inclinations, abilities, and efforts will take him.

Consider for the moment the role that salesmen have played in the development of our nation. America stands as the industrial giant of all times, not because she has more natural resources than the other nations of the world (she doesn't) but because she is the citadel of the free enterprise system where individual initiative is spurred forward by the profit motive. We've had our share of great industrialists, political leaders, scientists, and intelligent businessmen, but it's the salesman who has played the predominant role.

Salesmen play a crucial role in the economic life of our nation. Turning all our natural resources into products will serve no real purpose until these products are placed in the consumer's hands. A thousand printing presses stored in factory warehouses will not publish a single newspaper. A million board feet of lumber stacked in a lumberyard will not build a single house. These and all the other countless items produced in America must be moved by salesmen before they are of any use at all.

I have a close personal friend whose favorite expression is "Smoke comes out of factory chimneys in direct proportion to the words which flow from salesmen's mouths." He's right! It's the salesman who serves as the vital connecting link between a manufacturer's productive capacity and the consumer's ultimate utilization. The road building supplies and equipment, the tin cans and the machines which make and seal them, the automobiles, television sets, and radios, and all the other inventive creations which give our nation its high standard of living — all these things were placed in users' hands by salesmen. Salesmen introduced the product, created a desire for it, and then closed the sale.

Selling as a career

The opportunities which sales careers offer today are unparalleled in history. Our space age and its technology are moving forward so rapidly that tomorrow's salesmen will be selling thousands of products which have not yet been invented or even conceived of in man's mind. Just think of the untold number of selling jobs that are being created by scientific discoveries.

In short, a man who can sell will never have trouble making a living. A man who can sell well and sell professionally will not have to stop at the mere making of a living; he will be among our best paid and most respected professionals. Check the record. You'll find that the majority of top executives in America's major companies have progressed through the sales ranks to the top spots.

Selling makes society go!

Selling is the "go power" of our industrial society. It's not difficult to start a business if you have the necessary funds, but money and facilities alone will not put a business on its feet and keep it there. It's selling that makes our industrial world hum and without professional salesmen, performing with professional skill, our nation's economy would quickly grind to a halt.

And think of the materials the salesman uses in his creative effort. There's nothing as mundane as the clay of the sculptor, the paints of the artist, or the graphs and charts used by engineers. The modern salesman uses the strongest, most sensitive, most complex, and most fascinating material in all the world — the human mind. This is the raw material the salesman uses to create his livelihood and to transform prospects into customers.

Nor is age ever a handicap to the professional salesman. You can be at the start, at the midpoint, or even nearing the end of your sales career and you'll still have the opportunity to grow in professional stature.

Most men, at one time or another in their lives, wish for the opportunity of a fresh start, the opportunity to be reborn. A salesman has that opportunity *every day!*

Most of us, however, are so busy chasing the rainbow that we fail to take time out for reflection. We're so busy chasing that dollar that we don't take the time to step back and look at "the big picture." How often do we back away from our day-to-day problems and ask ourselves, "What can I do to improve my selling abilities?"

Please remember this! There's only one man in all this world who can hold you back from success. You can see this man by looking in a mirror.

If you have a sincere desire (and the courage) to use introspection, to look inward and analyze what you see, and to reorganize your selling habits, the following pages can be the most rewarding ones you've ever read. Just reading them, however, won't insure success. There's no magic wand involved. You'll have to use as well as understand the contents of these pages. You'll have to adapt them to your own individual sales program. This will take some thought, some planning, and some action: *your* thought, *your* planning, and *your* action.

Following the guidelines established by other professional salesmen is no guarantee of success. And it's doubtful that these guidelines will enable you to double or triple your sales overnight.

But you can expect to have new insight into yourself and your present selling program. And you can expect to become a better and more productive salesman. The guidelines are there and if you'll use them properly, the opportunity for success will be there, too!

The size of the business is limited only by the size of the man.

— *Elbert Hubbard*

Psycho-Sales-Analysis Guide

*After reading Section 2, write
your answers to these questions:*

1. If the world's best salesman had my present job, what
   would he be able to produce in:

   a. Sales volume?

   b. Personal income?

   c. Advancement opportunities?

2. What do I expect to produce in:

   a. Sales volume?

   b. Personal income?

   c. Advancement opportunities?

3. What are the *specific reasons* for the different answers
   I gave to questions 1 and 2 above?

4. Am I guilty of underestimating the potential of my
   present position? Explain fully.

5. What are the three most important reasons why I should
   keep my present job?

6. How would I rate myself *(poor, fair,* or *excellent)* in the
   following areas:

   a. Attitude toward my job.

   b. Enthusiasm.

c. Loyalty to my company.

d. Sales professionalism.

e. Service to customers.

f. Product knowledge.

g. Knowledge of my company.

h. Ambition.

i. Cooperation with my management.

7. Do I possess any negative attitudes which can be corrected to improve my performance, my income, and my enjoyment of my job? (No one is perfect, so be honest with yourself and lay these correctable traits out on the table where you can see them and do something about them.)

Section 3

Psycho-Sales-Analysis Guide

*Before reading Section 3, write
your answers to these questions:*

1. Am I proud of the product or service I sell? Why?

2. Do I have a step-by-step plan for selling my product?
   Name the steps.

3. What is the weakest point in my sales presentation?

4. What is the strongest point in my sales presentation?

5. Think of a less successful salesman in your field. Why
   is he less successful than you are?

6. Think of a more successful salesman in your field. Why
   is he more successful than you are?

7. How do I rate *(poor, fair,* or *excellent)* in these areas:
   a. Organization.
   b. Planning.
   c. Sales call preparations.
   d. Finding new prospects.
   e. Generating prospect interest.
   f. Overcoming objections.
   g. Closing the sale.

The golden stairway
to successful sales

Let's begin our consideration of basic sales techniques with a seldom discussed, but vital, element in salesmanship: the product or service being offered. To sell we should have something of value to exchange for the prospect's money. Too basic? Too simple? Absolutely not!

Years ago I held the imposing title of advertising manager for an association newspaper. The title was misleading. I managed nothing except myself for I was the newspaper's only salesman. I sold (or tried to sell) advertising space in the paper.

This newspaper's circulation was "controlled," which meant that the subscribers received the paper without paying directly for it. The newspaper was a "gift" when association members paid their dues to their association. And the purpose for the newspaper's existence was to publicize its side of a controversial subject.

I believed then, and I still believe, in the newspaper's program and the very wonderful people connected with that program. Still, the newspaper's contents were almost entirely educational, and I suspected (and knew in my heart) that readership was poor. Ads placed in the newspaper were seen and read by only a small percentage of the paper's large circulation. I knew this, and so did the potential advertisers, the people I was trying to sell.

The result? After a year of burning up the roads, knocking on advertising agency doors, and making a poor and unhappy sales record, I left the job. The product I was selling did not properly serve the prospects I was trying to sell it to. This newspaper's sales program was doomed from the very start.

There's a sequel to this story which proves that experience can teach. Some years later I was offered the position of sales manager with a newly organized company selling office supplies. Their markup was high. The quality of their products was low. In my discussions with the company president he made this statement: "Sure, I know our price is high and our quality's not the best. But that's the buyer's concern, not ours."

This company and I went our separate ways. The company was out of business within the year.

If you would not be willing to spend your own money for the product or service you are now selling (assuming you had your prospect's need), the greatest service you can do for yourself is to *change jobs today!*

A salesman needs integrity

It's true, you can make money selling products that have little or no value. You can use high pressure sales tactics and change towns often. But you'll be a peddler and not a salesman. Professional salesmen (men who have respect for themselves, their community, and the selling profession) must first have faith in the products they sell. A salesman without personal integrity can succeed only for a short time, if at all.

In addition to selling his product or service, a salesman also sells the company he represents. Will your company be in business tomorrow to back up the claims you've made for the product? Does your company have a history of dealing fairly with its customers? Are complaints handled promptly? Are your company's customers happy with both the product and the treatment they receive?

The finest product in the world will be difficult to sell if the company selling it does not support the product and the people who buy and use it. So if your answer to any of the questions in the preceding paragraph is no, I'll say again, *change jobs today!*

Now then, let's take a look at the basic selling steps used by successful salesmen since the beginning of time: The Golden Stairway to Successful Sales.

Step 1. Finding Better Prospects

Having a product or service to sell, it's obvious that the salesman's first step is to find a potential buyer.

You can, if you wish, follow the lead of most door-to-door salesmen and play the percentages. Knock on enough doors and sooner or later you'll find someone who will be willing to buy your product or service.

The problem here is that feet get tired, too many "no's" are discouraging, and days often end before minimum quotas can be reached.

Even in this form of selling the wise salesman plans his route. He knows that his chances of selling a $25,000 fork-lift truck will be better in the warehouse section of town than in the retail store area. Conversely, an $18 shopper's cart should sell more readily in the retail store area than in the warehouse district.

The importance of planning before making sales calls is seen in the careful selection of magazines and newspapers by mail order advertisers. "Calls" in the mail order business are made when the magazines with the company's advertisement are delivered to the subscribers. The key to success lies in selecting those publications which reach the largest number of people with the need for and the ability to buy the product or service.

Before ads are placed, the mail order expert (he's the professional in his field) studies the character of the magazine's readers. He knows in advance the average income and buying habits of the publication's readers. He knows their likes and dislikes, and he can tell you their average age, their distribution by sex, and the items they normally purchase by mail. When he carefully selects his prospects he is saving valuable advertising dollars.

Prospecting is equally important in direct sales. Regardless of the product or service being offered, the professional salesman will always plan ahead. He will try to conserve his time, save his steps, and put himself in the presence of well qualified prospects who have both the need for his product and the ability to buy it. With proper planning he's increasing his chances of making the sale more often, and to more people. These are the techniques we'll discuss in Section 4.

Step 2. Contacting the Prospect

After you've prospected and located your potential buyer, what's the best way to contact him? When? Where? If you're a salesman calling on a large corporation, who is the best man to see? Who can say yes instead of no to your proposition? These are the questions a professional salesman answers *before* he makes that first sales call.

If your product or service is not normally sold on the initial sales call, what intermediate goal should you try to accomplish on the first sales call? Should you telephone for an appointment or make a cold canvass call?

Different types of prospects respond differently to different sales approaches. The selling professional, the man who sells with his head instead of his feet, knows the right answers to these questions. He therefore makes his first contact easily, confidently, and successfully by using the techniques and procedures outlined in Section 5.

Step 3. Sparking Prospect Interest

Those first three minutes in the presence of a new prospect are perhaps the most crucial moments in the entire sales cycle. What you say and what you do on that first call can either open or close your prospect's mind. Your statements and your actions can also open or close the door of his office to future sales calls.

Successful salesmen use proved techniques to gain the prospect's attention, arouse his interest with provocative questions, and fix his attention on the product or service being sold. In Section 6 you'll have the opportunity to study the basic techniques used by professionals and with this background you will be able to interest more prospects in the merits of your product or service.

Step 4. Making the Prospect Want Your Product

Let's assume that you are a truck salesman who has made a prospect say to himself, "I hadn't thought about it before but I guess I would like to have a new truck." Now, how do you convince this prospect that *your* brand of truck is the one he should buy?

Professional salesmen talk specific benefits instead of reciting features. They know how to make proper demonstrations, follow basic sales patterns, and overcome competitive factors. After reading Section 7 you will know how to prepare your own preference-building presentations and be able to adapt them to different selling situations.

Step 5. Asking for the Order

Your prospect wants a product similar to yours and he's now decided that your brand is the one he should buy. How do you bring him to the point of signing that order?

For many centuries professional salesmen have used the proposal, either oral or written, to set the stage for their closing effort. This is perhaps the most often misunderstood basic in selling and its elimination from the sales cycle will almost always insure failure.

This step is sometimes described as a "trial close," a test to see if the prospect is ready to sign the order. It's also an easy, simple, and dignified way to ask for the order.

A recent survey by a national marketing magazine found that salesmen who *ask* for the order sell 300% more goods than salesmen who *wait* for the order. In Section 8 we'll look at ways professionals make their specific proposals and how you can add this important and necessary step to your own sales program.

Step 6. Closing the Sale

What should you do when you ask for the order and the prospect says no? What are the proven ways of capitalizing on the emotional temperament of a prospect? Here, in Step 6 of the sales cycle, we reach that moment of truth. It is at this point that many salesmen freeze and back away from the sale when the simple application of basic closing techniques would have completed the sale.

Is closing really difficult? If you believe that it is, you'll be pleasantly surprised to learn in Section 9 that you can become a more successful closer than you ever dreamed was possible simply by employing techniques known and used every day by the selling professionals.

The most important sales fact you'll ever learn

Please don't ignore the following statement. It's the most important fact you'll learn from this book:

The first six steps in The Golden Stairway To Successful Sales must be completed before the sale can be made.

Think about this for a moment. Have you ever completed a sale where these six basic steps were not involved?

It's admittedly true that the amount of time and effort spent on each sales step will vary widely with different sales situations. Yet each and every one of these six basic selling steps are present in every sale and must be completed before the sale can be completed.

Many times it's the prospect and not the salesman who initiates one or more of these basic sales steps. The man who walks up to the display booth at the Road Equipment Exposition and asks about the road grader that's on display has already (1) prospected himself, (2) initiated the contact, (3) aroused his own interest (or he wouldn't be there), and (4) may already have a partial preference for the brand exhibited in the booth. In this case the salesman can start midway in the sales cycle. But before the sale can be completed the salesman must finish the sales steps by strengthening the prospect's desire for this particular brand, (5) making the proposal for the prospect to buy, and (6) closing the sale.

Professional salesmen recognize the necessity and importance of these six basic sales steps. They know that each step must be finished (or partially so) before the next is attempted.

What happens when one of these basic steps is by-passed? If a prospect has no interest in road graders, will he want your brand? Is there any point in asking for the order? And if you fail to ask for the order, will the prospect buy? The answer in each case is — probably not.

It's basic, it's true, and it's a fact of business life. Each and every one of the first six steps in The Golden Stairway To Successful Sales must be completed in order for the sale to be consummated.

Step 7. Building Repeat Sales

The professional salesman knows that his job is not completed when the order is signed. Until the buyer is

A prospect who has not thought about owning a product faces a major decision when he's asked to buy.

It's a BIG STEP!

"No. I won't buy."

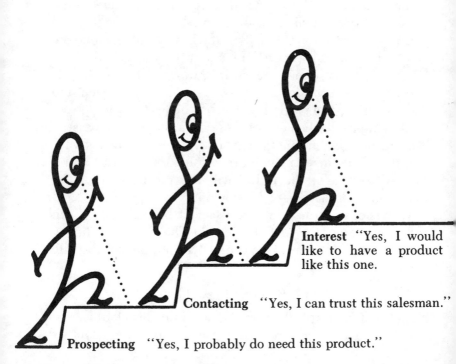

Interest "Yes, I would like to have a product like this one.

Contacting "Yes, I can trust this salesman."

Prospecting "Yes, I probably do need this product."

THE PSYCHOLOGY BEHIND THE
GOLDEN STAIRWAY TO SUCCESSFUL SALES

The same prospect finds it easy to make minor decisions as he is led up The Golden Stairway by an experienced salesman.

These are SMALL STEPS!

"Yes. I'll buy."

Close

Proposal "Yes, I know the salesman wants my order."

Preference "Yes, I prefer this brand over other brands."

actually using the product and is happy with his purchase, no sale is ever complete. Follow-up is a necessary function, both for good customer relations and for future orders.

How much follow-up is required? This will depend on the nature of the product or service being sold. The more technically complex the product or the higher its cost, the more need there is for proper follow-up after the sale.

And how should you handle customer complaints? How can you be fair to your customers, yourself, and your company when adjusting complaints? What's the best way to stay in contact with customers?

The answers to such questions are well known to the selling professionals. Section 10 will help you develop your own personalized follow-up program, set up and close multiple sales to the same customer, and gain the recognition and commensurate financial rewards that belong to selling professionals.

Selling as a profession

By now you'll have noted the many references being made to *professional* salesmen and the selling *profession*. Unfortunately, many who have failed as salesmen (as well as others who have never had the courage to try) are prone to scoff at the idea that selling should enjoy as much professional stature as the engineering or law professions. It is usually only those who have succeeded in this highly competitive field who are able to recognize the high degree of professionalism required for success.

Today, the art of selling is slowly but surely being transformed in the public mind from a trade to a profession. More and more colleges and universities are including selling and marketing courses in their curriculum. This, along with other indicators, should give heart to those who rightfully acknowledge selling as the intricate and studied art that it is.

Salesmanship stands today where engineering did in Europe prior to World War I. Herbert Hoover, who was instrumental in gaining true recognition for his fellow engineers, made this statement: "The European universities did not acknowledge engineering as a profession until long after America had done so. It was the American universities that took engineering away from the rule-of-thumb surveyors, mechanics, and Cornish foremen and lifted it into the realm of application of science, wider learning in the humanities with the higher ethics of a profession ranking with law, medicine, and the clergy."*

How does one solve this problem of attaining professional stature? Perhaps the most direct route is to follow Herbert Hoover's suggestion to "first determine the facts, arrange these facts in proper perspective, and then distill truth from them in the retort of experience."†

If you doubt that *basic* sales principles are important to experienced as well as inexperienced salesmen, consider Beech Aircraft Corporation's sales training program for its worldwide network of salesmen and sales managers.

Basic sales principles are universal

Can the same basic sales principles be used to sell a typewriter, a band saw, a case of tomato juice, and a $1-million airplane? Beech Aircraft not only says yes but also insists that all salesmen in their sales schools begin with *basic* sales techniques regardless of how many years they have sold airplanes or the degree of success they have already attained in the marketing field.

The experience level in each sales training class at Beech Aircraft Corporation ranges from new salesmen with as little

* *Memoirs of Herbert Hoover,* Vol. 1 (New York: The Macmillan Co., 1951). Reprinted by permission.

† Ibid. Reprinted by permission.

as 90 days of field experience to men who have successfully sold airplanes for many years.

"Even if you have worked out a highly successful sales program," these salesmen are told, "in the discussion of *basic* selling techniques you are likely to find one, two, or more ideas which will, at some future date, be responsible for the completion of a sale which could not have been made without this knowledge."

Professional salesmanship is based on an orderly progression of proven sales steps in a well-planned and well-executed selling program. Just as a military commander relies on progressive steps in his battle plan, the professional salesman plans and organizes his step-by-step "attack" in the battle for the consumer's order. This planning and organization, coupled with the proper use of basic selling techniques, is the mark of the selling professional.

Now that we've had the chance to look over The Golden Stairway, let's begin our climb by answering the next set of questions.

There are two necessities in doing a great and important work: a definite plan and limited time.
                                        — Elbert Hubbard

Psycho-Sales-Analysis Guide

*After reading Section 3, write
your answers to these questions:*

1. What are the seven progressive steps in The Golden Stairway to Successful Sales?

2. Which of the above sales steps am I now bypassing in my sales presentations?

3. Which of these sales steps are easy to accomplish?

4. Which steps are difficult to accomplish?

5. Recalling a recent successful sale, did I complete each of these basic sales steps?

6. Recalling a recent "unsuccessful sale," did I complete each of these sales steps?

7. If I am to become a more successful salesman, which of these sales steps require most of my attention?

Section 4

Psycho-Sales-Analysis Guide

*Before reading Section 4, write
your answers to these questions:*

1. Where am I now finding new prospects?

2. How many new prospects did I find and contact during
   the past year? This past month? This past week?

3. How do I now determine if a man (or business) is a
   legitimate prospect? What are my qualifiers?

4. How do I rate *(poor, fair,* or *excellent)* in these areas?

   a. Finding new prospects.

   b. Qualifying prospects.

   c. Following up on sales leads.

   d. Organizing prospect files.

   e. Keeping files current.

   f. Getting referrals from present customers.

5. What percent of contacted prospects become my
   customers?

6. What percent of my prospects are found by:

   a. Cold calls?   d. Research?

   b. Advertising?   e. Other?

   c. Referrals?

Finding better prospects

At the risk of oversimplification, it can be said that the very first problem faced by any salesman is how to locate the persons or firms who *might* buy his product or service. But trying to contact *all* the people who *might* buy your product is a herculean and, in most cases, impossible task.

The professional salesman recognizes that he, like every other man, has only 24 hours in each day. The more of these hours he can spend in face-to-face contact with legitimate prospects, the better his chances are of making sales. So the true professional refuses to rush blindly into calls on people who *might* buy and plans his sales calls on people who are *likely* to buy.

Who are the people most likely to buy your product or service? What makes a man you've never met a legitimate prospect instead of merely a "suspect"? It's a basic tenet of selling that before a man can be classified as a legitimate prospect he must possess three qualifying traits:

- The *need* for your product: Unless your prospect really needs the product you're selling, there's no valid reason for him to exchange his money for it.

- The *ability to buy* your product: Even if your prospect

needs your product he won't be able to buy unless he has the money to exchange for it.

- The *desire* for your product: The prospect may need your product and have the money to buy it. But he won't buy, and you won't be able to sell him, until he wants it.

Are there exceptions to these basic rules? The glib and handsome salesman who came into your home office and "sweet-talked" the purchasing agent into buying 550 reams of multicolored carbon paper he didn't need — is this an exception to the rule? Not really. Your purchasing agent felt at the time that he did have a need, or else he would not have signed the order.

But remember this: No sale is really complete until the customer is satisfied with the purchase. If your purchasing agent now feels he was taken in by the salesman's fast talk, that he didn't really need the multicolored carbon paper and now regrets his purchase, can you imagine the reception this salesman is going to receive on his next sales call at your home office?

Preselecting prospects

The man who sells merchandise where there is no need, no ability to buy, and no desire is not selling; he's peddling. This is a basic difference between professional salesmanship and peddlership. It is also the difference between making a good living and eking out a minimal living.

As the product being sold becomes more sophisticated or more specifically tailored to special needs, it becomes important for the salesman to spend more time and effort in preselecting his prospects. Magazines and pots and pans can be sold door-to-door because their use is almost universal. Atom smashers, scientific laboratory equipment, milling machines, and electronic data processing equipment have highly specialized markets and require thorough and extensive prospecting on the part of the salesmen. In short, if you are selling concrete mixers, you'll have to find out where the concrete users are.

Just because a man uses concrete in his business doesn't mean that he's a good prospect for a new concrete mixing machine. This man may have recently purchased a new concrete mixer and therefore doesn't have a *need* for a new one. Or, he may not have available funds and thus lacks the *ability to buy*. However, if he does use concrete in his business he is a better prospect than the man who never uses concrete. Your chances for creating desire with a user are much better than they would be with a nonuser. Simple and basic? Sure it is. But this is a basic sales principle that's often overlooked by the not-so-successful salesman.

Where might a concrete mixer salesman find better prospects? He'd probably find a "gold mine" in the membership list of the National Contractors Association. Directories of home builders, swimming pool contractors, and road builders would be other good sources.

Concrete mixers, calipers, cable, chemicals — the principle is the same. Regardless of the product you're selling there are some who are more apt to need your product than others. Finding these people requires only a small amount of imagination and ingenuity, and this effort can pay big dividends to you.

How much does it cost to make a sales call?

National sales organizations usually estimate the cost of an average sales call to be somewhere between $20 and $150 per call. If it costs you just $30 to make a sales call and you make five calls without a sale, you'll have to make a *net profit* of $180 on the sixth call (6 x $30) *just to break even!*

These are the economic facts of life known to every selling professional. This is why professional salesmen rely heavily on prospecting and qualifying prospects as to their (1) need, (2) ability to buy, and (3) desire for the product.

Find the common denominator

When prospecting, the professional salesman leans heavily on his knowledge of the people who have already purchased his product. What were their needs, abilities, and desires? Why did they make the decision to buy his product? If you'll find the "common denominator" of your present customers, you'll be able to narrow your search for other people who have similar needs, similar ability to buy, and similar desires. Such people are excellent prospects.

Keep prospect files current

Salesmen who have sold for a number of years will almost always have old prospect files gathering dust in the storeroom or on the closet shelf. How long has it been since you reviewed your records? Time has a habit of changing situations. Perhaps that prospect who wouldn't buy last year is no longer in business, but he could have more need and more reason to buy today than when you last contacted him. Reviewing old prospect lists *at regularly scheduled intervals* is a technique used by many professionals.

Set aside the last day of each month to review and update your prospect files. Why did you consider this man a prospect? Did he show any interest when you last called at his office? Why is he still on your active list? Has anything happened recently to change his need for your product? Is there a new and different approach you could use to sell this man? Regularly scheduled reviews of your prospect files can turn prospects into buyers. Try it!

Ask your customers to help

There's no doubt that "a happy customer is a salesman's best friend." Not only is word-of-mouth-advertising a decided asset, but a satisfied customer is often a very good source for new prospects. Have you ever thought about calling your present customers on the telephone, telling them that you're updating your prospect list, and asking them if they know anyone who might be interested in buying your product?

Asking present customers for prospect leads is a technique that has great psychological impact. It's strange but true — you can build stronger friendships by asking for favors than you can by doing them. If you doubt this, think of your own personal friends. If one of these people asked you to do him a favor, you'd know that he considered you a close friend. You'd be complimented, wouldn't you?

So don't hesitate to ask your customers for the names of others who might be willing to buy your products. Your customers will be complimented by your request.

Use all available information sources

If you sell for a living you should be thoroughly familiar with all the many reference books and periodicals available at the public library. Go to the library some evening and look around. Notice all the men browsing through trade directories, technical magazines, and reference books in the business or technical section. Chances are that many of these men are salesmen researching prospects, or checking out and qualifying sales leads.

Let's assume that you have the name of a company which is a "suspect." You feel this company might have a need for your product and the ability to pay for it. What does the company do? What does it manufacture or sell? Is it a financially strong company? Would the firm be a good credit risk? You can find the answers to these and to many other questions about this company in such reference books as: *Moody's Industrials, Dun & Bradstreet, Standard & Poor's* directories, the *Thomas Register*, the *Standard Directory of*

Advertisers, Chamber of Commerce directories, and state directories of manufacturers.

If you can't find the information you need, just ask the librarian. It's his job to help people find information and he enjoys doing this. You'll find that he, with his extensive knowledge of the library, will be able to direct you to many reference sources you probably haven't thought about. Newspaper clipping files, annual report files, out-of-town telephone directories, city directories, and other unexpected, but very valuable, reference materials are available for the asking by the polite and inquisitive salesman.

The library isn't the only place where information is maintained about local businesses. Bankers and stock brokers are often excellent sources. They know what's going on in their communities and who has the ability to buy your product. If properly approached, they'll be glad to help.

Don't forget those Chamber of Commerce officials in the cities and towns where you do business. Are there any trade or professional associations which make their headquarters in your town? Put on your thinking cap and you'll discover no end of places where you can find new prospects or qualify old ones.

New needs create new prospects

Some prospects are easier to find than others. But since they are easier to find, the chances are your competitors will already have found them. This is why many professionals, plagued by competition, do their prospecting in virgin territory. They use their imagination and ingenuity to ferret out new prospects, or they try to create a need for their product where none previously existed.

Let's illustrate "creative prospecting" by remembering our friend, the concrete-mixer salesman. If a man doesn't use concrete in his business, you say, there's not much chance of selling him a new concrete mixer. True!

But suppose you contact the owner of a brickyard. His salesmen are presently calling on building contractors who use concrete as well as bricks. You explain to this brick manufacturer how he can expand and diversify his product line by installing your ready-mix concrete plants around the state. You tell him about the extra profits he can make. You offer to help train his salesmen. You take this man out to visit a roofing manufacturer who successfully expanded his product line with your concrete plants.

Creative selling pays off

If you do your creative selling job properly, this brick manufacturer may decide to go into the concrete business. If he does he'll need concrete mixers, won't he? And who is going to have the first opportunity to sell him? *You are!*

Do you remember when grocery stores sold only groceries and drugstores sold drugs? Some creative salesman sold the then-new idea that profits were being missed by not selling stockings, cosmetics, beauty aids, and other products. This creative salesman started the rack industry.

When I was a boy my parents went to bookstores to buy books and toy stores to buy toys. Today, my wife often tucks a paperback novel into each sack of groceries, and frequently brings home a jigsaw puzzle with our aspirin.

Someone saw the potential. Someone sold the idea that books and toys could be profitably merchandised in grocery stores and drugstores. That someone, I'm betting, is now retired and enjoying the money he made as a creative salesman.

It's basic but true. If you can demonstrate a need you can usually sell the product, provided the prospect has the ability to buy and a desire for it.

Selling the need before selling the product does take time. Since the rent must be paid and the family fed, the professional salesman balances his missionary sales efforts with sales to people who already know they need his product. He pays his overhead by selling to his regular customers and other prospects who recognize their need for the product. Then he spends his extra time trying to create and demonstrate need to the "nonbelievers."

Successful insurance salesmen know they must have a constant supply of new customers if they are to survive in this highly competitive business. The initial commission is far larger than the renewal commission. So the insurance salesman simply cannot afford to spend all of his time calling on present customers. He must balance his sales calls to include a specific number of calls on new prospects each day or week.

Does this practice pay? It certainly does. Creative insurance salesmen are among the highest paid people in the selling profession.

Find new uses for your product and you'll find new prospects

Have you saturated your sales territory with the product you sell? Are your customers' warehouses and inventories full? Has your selling function degenerated into a dull routine of order taking? Then put on your thinking cap. Look around for *new ways* your product can be used. Other salesmen have done this and expanded both their sales horizons and their bank accounts.

Pressure-sensitive tape was first sold to manufacturers for sealing shipping cartons. The market was large but limited. Just look at the market today and see what creative salesmanship has done for the Minnesota Mining & Manufacturing Company and their famous 3M brand products.

You now find Scotch brand tape sold in every dime store, used in every type of industry and business, and stored in the kitchen drawer of almost every home in America. It's even sold to police departments because some creative salesman discovered that this tape could be used to lift fingerprints at the scene of a crime.

Japanese manufacturers of glass floats for fishing nets now sell these same floats to interior decorators. Acetylene torches made for shipbuilders are now sold to artists making "junk sculpture." A medicine-bottle manufacturer has expanded his line to include water bottles for bird and hamster cages. (These bottles, once 3¢, now sell for 26¢ in this specialized form.) These and countless other nonoriginal uses are selling products because a salesman used his eyes, his ears, and his head to be creative and find a new use for an old product.

Your company may already have a research staff that's responsible for finding new markets. But you're the man on the firing line. You're out in the field where the action is. Who stands to benefit the most from the discovery of a new product application? *You do!* So take the professional salesman's approach. Be creative in your prospecting, and reap the professional's reward.

Professional prospecting demands organization

If you now have a prospecting system that's working for you, fine and dandy. Please don't change it. But if you don't have a well organized plan and procedure for finding new prospects — get one. You can't grow in professional selling stature until you do.

Not everyone's a prospect

Are you sure you're able to recognize a qualified buyer for your product or service?

Not long ago I asked a very successful sales manager what, in his opinion, was the single biggest problem faced by his industrial paint salesmen. "Recognizing a prospect when they see one," he said.

He then went on to tell about a new salesman he had

hired. This salesman would rush from the office each morning and return late in the afternoon with complete and detailed records of his many sales calls. "He was making more calls than all our other salesmen put together," the sales manager said, "but he wasn't closing any sales. So one day I asked:

'How many sales have you lost?'

'None,' the salesman replied.

'I mean, how many of your prospects bought competitive brand paints?'

'None,' he said again.

'Then,' I said, 'you haven't been talking to legitimate prospects.'"

If you find that you are making a large number of calls for every sale, it would be well to ask yourself: "Am I making my calls on legitimate prospects? Do my prospects really need my product and do they have the ability to buy it?"

Good sales records are invaluable

Any discussion of prospecting would be incomplete without mention of the need for adequate prospecting records. The form isn't important and extensive detail isn't necessary. But you do need facts, and writing them down on paper will help you remember these facts and insure their instant availability when they are needed.

Many professional salesmen use their prospecting records to preplan as well as to record. They not only record what did happen, they also write down their plans for the follow-up sales call. These next-call, preplanning entries are made on the prospect card immediately following the sales call. This enables the salesman to make his next-call plans while the prospect's words, actions, and objections are still fresh in his mind. Try this simple technique. It's guaranteed to improve your effectiveness as a professional salesman and will put added dollars in your pocket.

What size record cards are best? It's a matter of personal choice. Three-by-five-inch cards are easy to file and can carry the basic information you'll need just before going into the prospect's office.

The important thing is to *write it down.* Don't trust it to memory. There can be many distracting events between the time you qualify your prospect and the time you make that sales call. Traffic lights, a chance meeting with a friend, and a good-looking girl passing by are commonplace distractions. So brief yourself by referring to your prospect card just before making that sales call. You'll be better prepared and more likely to make a successful contact, your next step in the sales cycle.

Don't sit down in the meadow and wait for the cow to back up and be milked — go after the cow.
                                        — Elbert Hubbard

Psycho-Sales-Analysis Guide

*After reading Section 4, write
your answers to these questions:*

1. What specific *needs* cause my present customers to buy my product or service?

2. What common financial status (ability to buy) do these present customers have? (Income, annual sales volume, etc.)

3. Where can I find new prospects with similar needs and the ability to buy?

4. How often should I review and update my prospect file?

5. Which customers should I contact and ask for additional sales leads? List by name.

6. Which reference manuals, trade publications, or other periodicals can provide me with the names of new prospects? If in doubt, ask your librarian.

7. Where can I create a new need for my product or service?

8. How many calls do I make for each completed sale?

9. How can I make more sales with fewer calls?

10. Do I have an organized prospect plan? Describe it.

11. How can my prospecting plan be improved?

Section 5

Psycho-Sales-Analysis Guide

*Before reading Section 5, write
your answers to these questions:*

1. What is my favorite method of contacting prospects?

2. Why is this method more effective than other methods of contacting I could use?

3. What different contacting methods are used by other salesmen in my field?

4. Why do these salesmen use different methods of contacting?

5. How do I rate *(poor, fair,* or *excellent)* in these areas?

   a. Getting appointments by telephone.

   b. Presentation organization.

   c. Getting appointments by letter.

   d. Obtaining immediate prospect interest.

   e. Persistence.

6. Whom (by title) do I try to see on the initial sales call to a new company?

7. What special preparations do I make for initial sales calls?

8. Which sales aids do I always carry for initial sales calls? What other sales aids should I carry?

How to contact prospects successfully

Now THAT you've uncovered a legitimate prospect, a company with the need for your product and the ability to pay for it, your first and immediate thought is to grab your sample case and go see them, talk to them, and *sell them!*

This reaction is a very natural one. You're certain this company is a bonafide prospect. You're full of drive and ambition. And in a way this is good. But the selling professional will always stand back and plan the attack before rushing blindly ahead. The old pro asks himself:

Who's the best man to contact in this company?

What's the best way to approach him?

Am I mentally prepared for this initial contact?

Do I have the information I need about this company?

Do I have a well-organized plan for this first sales call?

Deciding who to contact

The home door-to-door salesman has little trouble answering the who-should-I-contact question. His initial contact is made with the person who answers the door bell. If this salesman has a product normally purchased by women, he'll ask to see the lady of the house. He knows in advance that the lady of the house is the one best person to see. He has planned ahead.

Who can say yes?

If your product is normally purchased by the purchasing agent, your problem is equally simple. But many times, in selling to large organizations, the problem of who to see is not as easy to answer. Take, for example, the airplane business. Who in a large organization can say yes when you ask him to buy a $1 million airplane?

The traffic manager? This official is usually more interested in moving raw materials into the plant, and finished products out, than he is in transporting people. The traffic manager can give you a quick no, and as a general rule he has no authority to say yes.

The purchasing agent? This man works at the direction of others and someone else will probably have to approve the check for that $1 million airplane.

The comptroller? This man is the watchdog of the company treasury. He could issue the check but he won't want to. He is paid to say no. And he'll do just that, nine times out of ten, if you make a cold call request that he spend a large sum of money.

The president of the company, however, is interested in moving his key people about the country. He's interested in saving time and making money. He knows the entire company operation, not just a specialized segment. Most important of all, he's the top man — the only man who can say yes when you ask for the order.

From the above discussion you might conclude that airplane salesmen should always make their initial contact with the president of a company. While this is usually the case, there are exceptions.

If the company already owns a fleet of airplanes, there will be a chief pilot to consider. He is the company expert on air transportation. His recommendations can make or break the sale. If you go over his head and talk first with his boss, he certainly won't appreciate your action. So, which man should the airplane salesman see first, the president or the chief pilot?

There's no simple and easy answer to this question. The correct answer will be found only after the professional airplane salesman has done his homework thoroughly, studied the company's operation, and knows who does what in the company.

Here is the important thing to remember: regardless of the product you sell, there is an important psychological advantage in making your first contact as high as you can in a company's power structure. If you see the top man first and he refers you to one of his subordinates, you will have the top man's implied blessing. What subordinate would refuse to hear your story or give you a quick and unreasoned no when the top man himself has cleared your visit? Now you're dealing from a position of psychological strength.

It can be said that the higher the price tag on your product, the greater the need for you to contact the yes-man in the company. This is why the professional salesman is always asking himself: "Am I seeing the right people, the ones who have the authority to say yes to my proposition?"

About that first contact

Having decided on the individual to contact, the salesman's next problem is to select the contacting method most likely to prove successful. Should the salesman:

Call in person?

Telephone first for an appointment?

Write a letter asking for the appointment?

Ask a third party to arrange the appointment?

The salesman's goal, of course, is to insure that he will have the opportunity of sitting down knee-to-knee with the prospect to make a presentation. And the contacting method that will enable the salesman to do this is (for this salesman, this prospect, and this product) the best method of contact.

Is one of these contacting methods superior to the others? Let's look at some advantages and disadvantages of each.

Some contacting methods

Making that initial contact in person has one obvious advantage. The prospect, having admitted the salesman to his office, cannot very well deny him an interview. Many times, however, the prospect "isn't home" or has other pressing appointments and the salesman can't complete his cold call. Thus, calling in person isn't always the best method of contacting.

The salesman can elect to write a letter asking for an appointment. The advantage here is mostly psychological. "You are an important person — your time is important," the salesman implies when he writes for an appointment. The disadvantage of letters, of course, is that they are easily put aside or tossed into the wastebasket. Saying no to a letter instead of a salesman is a lot easier and a lot less embarrassing for the prospect.

Telephoning ahead for an appointment is also psychologically flattering to the prospect. But once again, it's much easier to say no over the telephone than it is in a face-to-face situation with the salesman.

When a professional salesman uses the telephone to gain appointments, he plans his conversation to avoid that fatal no. He always tries to leave the door open to further telephone calls. Failing to do this, the professional selling man may follow a telephone refusal with a letter which says: "I'll be in your area next week and will call at your office at 10 a.m. on Tuesday, May 10." He then makes an in-person follow-up call at the designated time on the designated date. This salesman has used a combination of three different approaches: telephone, letter, and personal call.

Perhaps the most important thing to remember about contacting is that there is no one best method. It's the method which works that's the best. And when one method of contacting doesn't work, *try another.* Don't give up until you succeed in getting that selling interview.

When working with more sophisticated products the use of third party referrals is often very effective. Here the technique is to allow some other person, one known to both the salesman and the prospect, to arrange for the sales appointment. This simple technique can often help the salesman get in the door when all other methods have failed.

The use of a third party's name when telephoning for an appointment is also a frequently used technique. "Jack Smith suggested I call you" is a phrase that can open the door to the office of Jack Smith's friend. Be sure, however, that you have Jack Smith's permission to use his name or this technique can backfire and kill the sale.

People's names are important

While we're discussing the use of names, please remember that it's important for you to know, use correctly, and remember the names of each of your prospects and customers. There's no sound in this world so sweet to a person's ears as the sound of his own name. The salesman who correctly pronounces Mr. Ito Yamacurita's name on the first sales call, spells it correctly in subsequent correspondence, and remembers it, is the salesman who has the best chance of selling Mr. Ito Yamacurita.

How can you be sure you're correctly pronouncing a prospect's name? That's easy. You can ask. You can ask the receptionist or the secretary before going into the prospect's office. You can ask the prospect himself. He's not going to be insulted. He's going to be complimented because you have enough genuine interest to want to say his name correctly.

Memory experts tell us that we only forget the names of people who are unimportant to us. We've all stood in long reception lines, acknowledging introductions with a hand-shake and a smile, and then forgotten the names within the next five minutes. But if that reception line included six people whom we recognized as potential buyers of our product, would we remember those names? You bet we would!

Robert F. Hudson, well-known management consultant, said it well: "I've never met a *good* salesman yet who didn't know my exact name, how to spell it, and my title as well."

If you have trouble remembering names, take time out to do something about this professional deficiency. There are many good books on the subject. There are memory courses that can be taken for a nominal fee. You cannot afford to be less than near perfect in the art of remembering names.

Persistence pays

How effective and how necessary is the element of persistence? A nationwide survey of sales executives and sales managers produced these very interesting figures: 48% of their salesmen made one call and stopped; 25% of their salesmen made two calls and stopped; 12% of their salesmen made three calls and stopped; 15% of their salesmen made more than three calls.

And who do you suppose sells most of the merchandise? You're right. This same survey reported that 80% of all sales were made after the fifth call.

The conclusion — *15% of the salesmen (the professionals) make 80% of the sales.* Persistence does pay off!

Be prepared

When planning an initial contact, professional salesmen always have a secondary as well as a primary goal. Their primary goal, of course, is to sell their product or service. However, the nature of that product or service may be such that first-call sales are the exception rather than the rule. Electronic computers, power generating plants, heavy mining machinery, and other "high ticket" items usually require many calls before a sale can be made. Thus, the professional salesman, on this initial call, will almost always plan a secondary objective. And this objective is firmly fixed in his mind before the contact is made.

The salesman may, for example, ask for permission to study the prospect's present bookkeeping system to see how an electronic computer might save time and money for the firm. Or he may want to take the prospect on a tour of a mine to show him how others are using the mining machinery he sells. The professional plans ahead and has a set objective for each call. This includes the initial contact.

There's a close parallel to be found in the field of aviation. The pilot of an airliner is required to file a written flight plan before each flight. He must not only write down his destination but an alternate destination as well. This is to make sure that the flight will be completed safely in case the weather turns sour and prevents him from reaching the original destination.

Professional salesmen also have alternate destinations. If they cannot close the sale on the initial sales call, they will attempt to reach an intermediate objective, one which leaves the door open for further calls or sets up an appointment for a demonstration. Professionals know where they want to go. They plan their course of action, and they arrive at their predetermined goals.

First contacts are important

As every professional salesman knows, the first few minutes in a prospect's office are vitally important. This is the time when the salesman must set the stage for the sale and establish the selling climate. This is also the time when the salesman gains or loses the confidence of the prospect.

If the initial contact is to be successful, the salesman must reflect, in his statements and in his actions, a genuine liking for the man he is attempting to sell. Animosity, superiority, or just plain disinterest are feelings a prospect can sense instantly. These are also feelings which can quickly destroy the salesman's chances of completing the sale.

Today's selling professional knows that the horse-and-buggy methods of yesterday — the glib chatter, back slapping, and checkered-suit salesmanship — will not enable him to survive in today's competitive business climate. So, instead of relying on trick statements to make that all-important first impression, today's salesman attempts to serve his prospect and win his confidence. He gains the prospect's interest and respect by earning them.

If you'd like to establish selling rapport on that initial sales call, just follow these four proven guidelines:

- Prove that you know something about the prospect's business and problems.
- Give the prospect a chance to talk and participate in the selling situation.
- Think before you talk. Never make quick, unconsidered remarks.
- Make certain the prospect understands (and agrees with) the things you are saying.

Men who make money in the selling profession never play "king of the mountain"; they let the prospect stand alone on a pedestal. After all, the prospect is the most important person in the salesman's professional life. So, the professional salesman always lets his prospect know, by actions and by words, that he likes him, understands his problems, and is there with the sole objective of helping him solve his problems. The salesman tries to establish this all-important relationship on that initial sales call.

You'll also find that the professional salesman keeps small talk and chitchat to a minimum. His prospect is a busy man. Time is important to both of them. Unless the salesman knows the prospect is really eager to talk about such things as golf or fishing, the selling professional quickly gets to the purpose of his sales call. By showing respect for the prospect's time, a salesman can always set himself up as a professional in the eyes of the prospect, and consistently get more orders than the salesman who wastes time by overplaying the I-like-your-hobby-too role.

The eyes and the voice — a salesman's best friends

Nothing can establish mutual confidence, respect, and friendliness faster than eye-to-eye contact. Watch two old friends conversing. You'll find them talking with their eyes as well as their voices. There's warmth and understanding when their eyes meet. Why? Because neither person has anything to hide from the other. They are not afraid to peer into each other's innermost thoughts.

One of the most successful salesmen I know has made it a habit to look into the eyes of each new prospect and note their color. He can tell you the color of the eyes of every customer he has from Georgia to Maryland. If you doubt the tremendous power of this simple technique, try it! I'll guarantee you're in for a most pleasant surprise.

The voice, too, can command immediate interest and establish a proper selling climate more rapidly than you ever imagined. Macy's, the famous New York department store, is reported to have run an interesting experiment which proves this point. The store asked its employees to emphasize the word *morning* when they said "good morning" to their customers. This upward inflection put more excitement into the salesmen's voices, caused a noticeable warm-up in the customers, and helped increase the daily sales volume.

It's possible, of course, to go overboard when you use your voice. Yelling is not selling, and you can be so loud in talking that a reverse effect occurs and the prospect resents your presence.

The frosting on the cake of your greeting is a smile. Make it a habit to smile when you say "good *morning*." Smile and your customers will smile back while they sign the order.

The six cardinal sins when contacting

Throughout my years of conducting sales training classes I have collected, along with many "what-to-do's," a number of "what-not-to-do's" for salesmen making their initial sales contact. These represent the findings of highly successful salesmen and I'd like to share them with you:

Please don't waste your prospect's time with an unorganized presentation. No one likes to sit through a movie in which the plot is a mishmash of disjointed and unrelated actions. Prospects are human, too. They become bored, disinterested, and downright unfriendly with salesmen who are disorganized. They feel the salesman is wasting their time — and he is! He's also wasting his own time because uninterested prospects don't become interested customers.

Please don't insist that your golden voice be allowed to intone on and on, uninterrupted. Suppose you're in full voice and going strong when the prospect interrupts with a question. Sure, you'd like to continue and finish that well-practiced sales pitch. But resist the urge! A prospect's question is a sign of interest. It might be a sign that he's ready to buy. Be thankful for that kind of interruption.

Please don't smoke without an invitation from the prospect. The smell of cigarettes, pipes, and cigars is often offensive to nonsmokers. Besides, the number of reformed smokers and anti-tobacco evangelists is increasing daily due to the surgeon general's report. Smoking without an invitation to do so in another man's office is not only ill-bred, it's foolish. Could you expect to sell your product while sipping martinis at a WCTU picnic?

Please don't use the prospect's first name without his invitation to do so. Sure, you want to get on a first-name basis with him as soon as possible, but let him make the first move. If he wants to lower the formal barriers, he'll let you know in due time. Don't rush him; it could cost you a sale.

Please don't be insensible to your prospect's mood. You have your bad days. So do your prospects. If your prospect is obviously agitated and sour on the world, the worst thing you can do is to barge into his office and start telling jokes.

Please don't lose your dignity and poise. You can't afford to let unexpected questions and unusual actions throw you. Prospects will often try to push you off balance. Don't let them. Stand back and think before you reply. Smile while you're thinking. Maintain your dignity and poise and you can overcome any unexpected turn of events.

In the final analysis, successful contacting requires knowledge of a few simple contacting techniques and procedures plus a great deal of persistence. The other ingredient for success is the application of that knowledge in your own well-organized contacting program.

So let's get organized now by taking pencil in hand and answering the follow-up questions on the next page.

Genius is only the power of making continuous efforts. A little more persistence, a little more effort, and what seemed hopeless failure may turn into glorious success. There is no defeat except from within, no really insurmountable barrier save our own inherent weakness of purpose.

— Elbert Hubbard

Psycho-Sales-Analysis Guide

*After reading Section 5, write
your answers to these questions:*

1. Am I seeing the right prospects, the ones who can say yes when I ask for the order?

2. Which of the four contacting methods could I use in my personal sales program?

3. On the average, how many sales calls do I make to get one order?

4. Who (by name) are three good prospects I have *not* been able to see?

5. What methods of contacting should I now use to contact the three prospects I listed above?

6. What are three questions I can use to get my prospects to talk about their businesses?

7. On initial sales calls, what are my:

    a. Primary objectives?

    b. Secondary objectives?

8. Which product benefits should I try to cover in the first three minutes of an initial sales call?

Section 6

Psycho-Sales-Analysis Guide

*Before reading Section 6, write
your answers to these questions:*

1. Why should a prospect allow me to come into his
    office? (If I don't know the answer to this question, I
    shouldn't be calling.)

2. How do I now try to get the prospect's attention?

3. How do I now hold the prospect's attention?

4. What visual aids do I use on:

    a. Initial sales calls?

    b. Follow-up sales calls?

5. Why should a prospect give more time and consideration
    to me than he does to my competitors?

6. Thinking back to a prospect who wouldn't let me make
    a second call:

    a. Why did the prospect feel this way?

    b. What could I have done to change his attitude?

7. What questions do I usually ask on initial calls?

8. Remembering my most successful first call, why was
    the call so successful?

How to spark prospect interest

Every experienced salesman can recite stories about the prospect who literally took the product away from him. In the automobile business there's "the farmer who came into the showroom, pulled out a roll of bills big enough to choke a horse, and bought the red convertible." Or the plant manager who told the conveyor salesman, "I've been waiting for you to call"; the purchasing agent who "just ran out of typewriter ribbons and demanded six gross." These are familiar stories in the selling profession.

Oddly enough, many of these stories are true. Sadly enough, they do not occur with sufficient frequency to make selling an easy and effortless task. Nor will these unusual sales pay the rent or buy the groceries for the average salesman.

It doesn't take a great deal of thought to realize that if a prospect needed your product, had the ability to buy your product, and wanted your product, *he'd already have your product.* Thus, in 99 and 44/100% of the cases, the element of desire will have to be implanted by the salesman. And a prospect can't have desire until he has interest.

It should be mentioned that the basic steps in selling often overlap. The salesman who preceded his initial sales call with a letter and a brochure describing his product has already tried to create interest in the mind of his prospect. The salesman who telephones and makes an appointment has already generated some interest or the prospect would not have agreed to an interview. However, this preliminary interest in the product must be strengthened during the first few minutes of the sales call. If it isn't, the salesman is going to find himself on the outside of the office, wondering what happened.

The point we're making is this: If a prospect isn't interested in a product, he will not develop desire and cannot be sold. And if the salesman can't generate interest on his first call, there probably won't be any follow-up calls. So, the important interest step on The Golden Stairway to Successful Sales must be nailed down quickly and early in the sale.

Mink coats or Volkswagens?

What can you do to arouse interest on the first sales call? What can you say or do to command the prospect's attention and glue his eyes and his ears to your sales message? The answer is to appeal to interests already held by the prospect. But how do you discover these interests?

An oil company president whose wife wears mink coats and diamond bracelets, and who belongs to the country club and drives expensive automobiles, is probably interested in prestige. A furniture manufacturer who drives a Volkswagen and buys his clothes at Robert Hall would be interested in economy. A businessman who has just installed a new data processing machine in his ultramodern plant will probably respond favorably to a discussion of your product's efficiency.

What benefits and features does your product have that would appeal to these different people and their different interests? Talk about the benefits you believe will match their interests. Watch for signs of interest and concentrate on those benefits which appear to be gaining the prospect's attention.

How, you ask, can a salesman discover in advance the probable interests already held by his prospect? The answer lies in research and observation. For if you have prospected and qualified your prospect properly (Step 1 in The Golden Stairway), you will have discovered a great many things that will help you sell him.

Know your prospect

In-depth researching can tell you many things about the large business or corporation you are trying to sell. Looking through reference books and talking with your banker can give you much of the essential information you need about the prospective customer's size and financial strength.

At the other end of the spectrum, when selling to individuals and smaller companies, you will probably have to rely on personal observation. How is the prospect's office decorated? How is the man dressed? What sort of pictures are hung on his office walls?

Would you like to sharpen your powers of observation? It's not difficult to do. Just take a magazine picture and write down all the facts you can determine or guess about the people in the picture. Are these the type of people you'd expect to find at the baseball game or at a symphony concert? Would these people know how caviar tastes or would they be more familiar with corned beef and cabbage? You'll be surprised at how quickly you can learn to "size up" prospects.

Don't, however, rely solely on your newly acquired abilities to determine interests solely by observation. Don't decide that this particular prospect is the economy type, and talk and talk about economy to the exclusion of all other benefits. You're apt to talk yourself into a corner.

Test your personal observations by mentioning the benefit you *think* will interest this prospect and then watch for his reaction. If the mentioned benefit doesn't seem to be doing the job — if the prospect seems bored or uninterested — change your approach. Talk about another type of benefit and watch for his reaction. Keep changing benefits until you strike pay dirt. Then expand on that benefit.

Sell people instead of products

Professional salesmen realize that they are not selling a product or service, they are selling *people*. Since people have different likes and dislikes, different goals and ambitions, different needs and different wants, no single benefit or single approach will spark the interest of every prospect.

A professional salesman is much like a fisherman who has studied his fishing hole, knows where the fish are located, and when one lure doesn't work, changes to another. A fisherman who knows the location, habits, and probable food choice of fish will always catch fish. A salesman who knows people, researches or observes their individual interests, and uses different "lures" to fit those interests, will always be able to arouse the interest of his prospects.

Help the buyer sell himself

On initial sales calls, most professional salesmen try to entice their prospects into participating in the sales effort. It has been said that nothing worthwhile ever happens until someone gets excited. This is particularly true in selling. The sales professional knows that he will have to:

- Get the prospect's attention.
- Get the prospect to listen to the sales story.
- Get the prospect to identify his own personal needs and wants, and relate them to the benefits the product or service offers.

Once these things are done, the sale is nearly made. Now let's talk about how this can be done.

Every salesman, like each of his prospects, is an individual in himself. His background, his personality, his education, and his likes and dislikes make him a unique person. In all this world there is no other person who has the same basic character traits, the same physical features, the same mental outlook, or the same view of life. Each man, in his total of characteristics, is as unique and different as his fingerprints. Thus, the things which will arouse interest in one man may fail miserably when you try to use them to arouse interest in another.

In short, there is no *one* best way to arouse interest. If there were a best way, every prospect would be approached in the same manner with every salesman using his one best approach. So, the problem becomes one of each salesman experimenting with different methods of creating interest in his product or service until he finds the one method which works best for him.

Here are some of the proven methods used by professional salesmen:

Do the unexpected

Almost everyone is familiar with the favorite interest-arousing technique of the vacuum cleaner salesman. He dumps a pile of dirt on the rug at the start of his demonstration and says, "Don't worry, Madam, our Little Gem vacuum cleaner will have this mess cleaned up in a hurry."

What happens? The dismayed prospect is horrified at the sight of all that dirt on her rug, worried that the vacuum cleaner won't do the promised job, but understandably relieved when it does. She's a captive audience since she's not about to go off and leave the demonstration until she's sure the dirt has been completely removed from her rug.

A good friend of mine makes himself, instead of his product, the object of prospect curiosity. Paul is recognized as one of the world's best roofing salesmen. Since there is little glamour in his product, he often focuses attention on himself by carrying carrots in his pockets and offering to share a bite with his prospects.

"They never forget me or my product," says Paul when asked about this unusual attention-gaining device. Bizarre? Unconventional? Sure it is! But while this method of gaining the prospect's attention probably won't work for the man who sells locomotives, aluminum extrusion machines, or other high cost items, the techniques does work well for Paul and has enabled him to build a highly successful roofing business on the West Coast.

How unusual should you get? This depends entirely on you, your product, and your prospects. Please don't try to use attention devices that are out of character with you and your personality. You must be yourself (people these days call it "doing your own thing"). But if you can capture the prospect's attention with the unusual or unexpected (provided it doesn't offend him or let him mentally classify you as a "nut") he'll listen to your sales story.

Shock with a true statement

"Do you realize, Mr. Jones, that more than $250,000 is made and spent by the average American in his lifetime?"

What happens when you ask a shoe manufacturer this question? His first thought is probably something like this: "I wonder how much of that $250,000 they spend on shoes?" Or he may do some mental gymnastics to total the amount of money *he* expects to make in *his* lifetime. (Isn't it exciting when we discover that we're more successful than the average man?) This question, or one like it, will not only get the prospect's attention, but will start his mental participation in the sale.

Or, you might ask this shoe manufacturer, "Were you aware, Mr. Jones, that this machine will increase your production by exactly 12%?" What happens? Mr. Jones isn't going to let you get away with making such a positive statement and he'll challenge you to prove it. You have his undivided attention. And now that you have his attention, prove your statement, and you'll have the sale half completed.

Is there an unusual or little-known fact about your product that you can use as an opening statement? Think about this and you'll probably be able to come up with several such facts. Work them into provocative and challenging statements. Try them out on different prospects. Select the one that seems to work best for you. You'll be surprised at how this simple technique can hold the door open and gain the time you need to establish a good selling rapport, tell your sales story, and complete the sale.

Challenge with questions

Instead of using a dramatic, true statement, many professional salesmen prefer to challenge the prospect with a series of questions. This technique has the advantage of requiring verbal response on the part of the prospect. He's forced into becoming an active participant in the selling situation.

Consider this series of questions used by a data processing equipment salesman and the answers of his prospect, who has never owned a computer:

Salesman: Do you use adding machines in your office, Mr. Johnson?

Prospect: Why yes, I do.

Salesman: Are they *electric* adding machines?

Prospect: Of course.

Salesman: Why don't you use *manual* adding machines, Mr. Johnson? They're much less expensive.

At this point the prospect's interest has been indirectly

focused on the importance of saving time. This happens to be the very product benefit the salesman wants to talk about. Through questions and answers this salesman has centered his prospect's thoughts on the subject at hand — how computers can save time for his company.

Ask key questions

A good house-to-house salesman will ask a housewife questions about her home, get her talking about that small corner of the world that's exclusively *hers*. "You thoroughly enjoy your home, don't you. Mrs. Smith?" This type of key question will generate the necessary prospect interest and participation for salesmen offering rugs, furniture, books, or potato peelers.

This same technique works wonderfully well in the industrial sales world. Ask a businessman about his business. This is perhaps the most important thing in the businessman's life, his family excluded. Ask him how his business operates; mention that you saw an article about his company or business in a trade magazine; get him to talking about the things that interest him. Then key the benefits of your products to those interests.

Start the prospect talking and the chances are he'll supply you with sales ammunition you can use later on in the sale. If he brags a bit about the percent of net profit he makes on his invested capital, this is your cue to show him how your machine helped another manufacturer make an extra 2% on his invested capital.

Questions are an excellent method of arousing prospect interest in a custom-made product. This is because the product that will eventually be sold is not as yet in final form. The customizing of the product may add or subtract from its benefits. So, the wise salesman will question at length regarding the customer's specific needs, wants, and desires.

As a general rule, it can be said that selling customized products requires more participation by the prospect and less participation by the salesman. Selling a custom-made product? Then ask questions. There's no better way to generate prospect participation in the sale.

Key questions are those that bring a "yes" response. They get the prospect into the habit of saying yes, and that's exactly the answer you'll want when you get around to asking for the order.

Use words the prospect understands

When a salesman talks he should be more concerned with the connotation of his words in the mind of the prospect than in their dictionary definitions. The reaction a prospect will have to a word, negative or positive, will not depend on its definition; it will depend, instead, on the personal connotation the prospect places on the word.

Professor Richard D. Altick, who teaches English at Ohio State University, writes: "Personal connotations are the result of the experience of the individual man or woman. The way we react to ideas and objects, and thus to the words that stand for these 'referents,' is determined by the precise nature of our earlier experience with the 'referents.' "*

"More than 35,000 teachers use our visual aids equipment" is a statement which may or may not arouse interest. It all depends on the image of teachers which the prospect holds in his own mind. If the prospect likes teachers, respects them, and holds their opinions highly, this would be a good interest-arousing statement. However, if the prospect was expelled from school and dislikes teachers, the statement could evoke a negative and unwanted response.

As a general rule, it is wise to talk in the simplest possible terms with your prospect. If you're selling to doctors,

---

* *Preface to Critical Reading,* 5th edition (New York: Holt, Rinehart and Winston, Inc., 1968).

chemists, or electrical engineers, you'll no doubt be using many technical terms which are well understood by these professionals. If, on the other hand, you use these same technical terms when talking to laymen you'll immediately be classified as a "stuffed shirt" or a "show-off."

Please remember that your objective when selling is to communicate an idea. Any language which detracts from the objective can prevent you from reaching your goal. Edward J. Hegarty, director of sales training for Westinghouse Electric Corporation, makes the following suggestion: "The simplest way of saying a thing is best. Instead of removing your hat, take it off. Don't accompany your boss, go with him; don't return, come back; don't accomplish things, do them; don't ascertain, find out; don't utilize, use. A lot of words you use every day can stand simplification. You say that none of these longer words are difficult, and you're right, but the substitutes are simpler, aren't they?"*

Use mechanical devices and visual aids to increase your sales

Professional salesmen never discount the power of the factory produced sales aid, the brochure and other printed literature, the chart and graph visuals, photographs, models of the product — the list is almost endless. Why sell with your bare hands when information and demonstration sales aids are so readily available for your use?

All of us are, upon occasion, fascinated with the sound of our own voice. In the bathroom shower this is fine and acceptable. But long, uninterrupted monologues will quickly bore any prospect. If all you do is talk, all the prospect can do is listen. The alternative? Show something while you talk. Now the prospect can not only hear but can also see what you're talking about.

* *Making Your Sales Meeting Sell* (New York: McGraw-Hill Book Co., 1955). Reprinted by permission.

Give your prospect's ears a rest and let him use his eyes. He'll then be using two instead of only one of the communications devices nature provided. If you'll let your prospects use their eyes and ears, you'll double your chances of building interest in your product. And don't forget those other sensing devices mother nature gave us. If you can, let your prospect feel, taste, and smell the benefits of your product or service. (This is why used-car salesmen spray the insides of their jalopies with "new car smell." And it really works!)

A salesman may not be able to use all the many factory sales aids available to him. But he should keep an open mind. *Someone* thought the sales aid would help. *Someone* is offering an idea he might use. *Someone* could possibly be a bit smarter than the salesman about this one particular sales approach. Self-confidence is great. But don't let it close your mind to innovations which can help you grow in professional selling stature. Percy Bridgman* expressed this idea very well:

> *There's no excuse except sheer stupidity*
> *against the impact of a new idea.*

Have you ever given thought to the "blood, sweat, and tears" which are expended by professional advertising men in the preparation of product brochures and advertisements? Each word is carefully chosen for its impact. Each phrase is designed to evoke emotion or urge action on the part of the reader. These same words can be adapted to your selling program.

When you receive that new factory brochure, study the provocative statements and questions in the big, bold headlines. These words are arranged in order according to time-tested formulas. These words stop the reader and lead

---

* United States physicist and Nobel Prize winner (1882-1961).

him to the smaller print in the body of the advertisement or the inside of the brochure. These very same words can be used by you to create interest, hold attention, and lead the prospect to the conclusion that he should buy your product.

Professionals in the selling world read every word in every ad about their product and competitive products. They recognize that these words were placed in the ad by professional copywriters, the "word salesmen" employed by the advertising agency. So professional salesmen wisely borrow phrases, carry ads with them on sales calls, and often show the prospect underlined statements in the ads to strengthen their sales presentations.

While we're on the subject of arousing interest, do you remember the speaker who was "glued" to the rostrum at the last Rotary Club meeting? Wouldn't that speaker have held your interest more easily if he had occasionally moved away from the speaker's stand? Wouldn't you have listened more intently if he'd departed once or twice from his prepared presentation? Sure you would!

Advertising professionals tell us that counter displays which move are seen twice as often and are twice as effective as displays which are immovable. A motionless, sit-in-the-chair, talk-only salesman is trying to hold his prospect's attention the hard way.

Show testimonials — they're terrific interest builders

There's a bit of the competitive spirit in each of us and prospects are no exception. Every businessman is intensely interested in how his competitors operate their businesses. Every purchasing agent is curious about the supplies his counterpart down the street is buying. So, take advantage of testimonials. They can be a big help in capturing the prospect's interest.

Collect and use written or printed testimonials by people who are happily using your product or service. There's no better way to open the mind of a prospect than to show him, in black and white, and preferably with pictures, how his competitors feel about your product.

Listen to those prospects

Inexperienced salesmen often become so absorbed in what they are trying to tell the prospect that they fail to listen to what the prospect is trying to say. The result? A breakdown in communications. And without communications, the two-way type, there can be no continuing interest.

Professional salesmen also know that there's a big difference between listening and understanding. They recognize the critical importance of not only *hearing* the prospect's words but also *understanding* his intent.

What the prospect says and what he means are not necessarily one and the same. At least, the prospect's intent and the salesman's interpretation of this intent are frequently different. Many times this communications breakdown is caused by the salesman overlooking the emphasis a prospect places on his words. If you doubt that emphasis plays an important role in the communications process, take this sample statement:

I never said I needed this product.

At first glance this seems to be a simple, straightforward statement which could not be misunderstood. But now, stress the italicized word in each of the following sentences and notice how the meaning of the sentence changes:

"*I* never said I needed this product."
Translation: Someone else may have said they needed this product, but *I* didn't.

"I never *said* I needed this product."
Translation: Sure, I may need this product or implied that I needed it, but I didn't say so.

"I never said I *needed* this product."

Translation: I may want the product but I haven't admitted this fact.

There you have it, the same sentence with different meanings. See how easy it is to change meaning and intent simply by stressing different words!

Dr. Irving J. Lee, professor of public speaking at Northwestern University, writes about a class experiment in which "the listener was asked to write in his own words a 50 word abstract or summary of what a speaker said. Only rarely would the speaker (after a study of the abstracts) report that more than 25% of the class adequately 'got it.' They reported something but it was not his idea as he gave it. If the audience heard they did not seem to listen. Or if they listened it seemed with half an ear."*

Prospects seldom have the same keen interest in buying a product that the salesman has in selling it. Consequently, the limited attention a prospect may give to the salesman's words may lead to misunderstanding. The professional selling man knows he must listen for the emphasis placed on words and the inflections in the prospect's voice. He knows that trying to understand the prospect's meaning along with his words is going to take a 100% listening effort.

Give your prospects a fair hearing. Give them all the attention you expect them to give you when you are the speaker. Communication, the prudent salesman knows, is a two-way street.

Put yourself in the prospect's shoes

If you were a prospect for the product you're selling, what features and benefits would interest you? This is a relatively easy question to answer.

---

* *How to Talk With People* (New York: Harper & Row, Inc., 1952).

Now put yourself in the prospect's place. Can you be sure that the things which interest you will also interest him? You can't be sure.

What you believe to be an important benefit has absolutely no bearing whatsoever on the sale. It's the way in which your prospect views the benefit that makes it important or unimportant. It's his evaluation, not yours, that can make or break the sale. As one of my manufacturing agent friends says, "You sometimes have to think like a prospect in order to sell one."

Thinking like a prospect isn't nearly as difficult as it sounds. If you have researched your prospect properly you will have uncovered a number of things about him. You'll know something about his needs and his ability to buy. You'll be able to use this background information to decide which product benefits should interest him. Talk about these benefits first. Watch his reaction as you talk. When you do locate his area of interest, expand and develop those benefits.

Invite the prospect to talk

There will be times when your prospect begins to lose interest in spite of all your efforts. He may yawn. He may turn in his chair and look out the window. He may begin to fidget and squirm in his seat.

When this happens, it's time for you to trade places with the prospect. Put him in the speaker's role. Ask him a direct question that requires a direct answer — one that can't be answered with a simple yes or no. A man who is busy answering your question is not apt to be daydreaming about other things.

Questions are one of the most powerful weapons in the salesman's arsenal of procedures and techniques. Questions require a prospect to participate actively in the sale. Questions help the salesman learn his prospect's hidden wants and needs. Questions can give the salesman time to regain lost composure. Yet many salesmen prefer to do all the talking. They're so intent on telling their story that they never give the prospect a chance to talk. Questions, these salesmen seem to fear, will break the continuity of their memorized presentation.

If you find that your prospect is not paying proper attention to your sales story, relax a bit. Slow down. Ask a question and get your prospect to talk. Chances are, he'll welcome this change of pace (and the opportunity to express *his* views) and end up by selling himself on your proposition.

Make certain your prospect knows you're there to help him

There's a hard school of salesmanship that considers selling an exciting game of wits. "It's like a chess game," a salesman says. "I find a man with money and invite him to sit down and play the game. My goal is to make him part with his money. His goal is to make me keep my product.

"I say this and he counters by saying that. I move with benefit presentations and he countermoves with objections. It's move and countermove until one or the other of us is checkmated and the sale is made or lost."

A lot of salesmen play the "game" this way. Some of them are successful — most of them are not. Why? The reason is obvious. Very few prospects will be interested in playing a game in which their opponent is more skilled than they are. The prospect has his own problems and needs that require filling; he isn't interested in playing games. He wants to deal with salesmen who can help him solve the problems that plague him. He'll be interested in buying from salesmen who are interested in fulfilling needs.

If you want to generate interest in both yourself and your product, convince the prospect that his needs and wants are uppermost in your mind. Your primary and only reason for calling on him is to help him, not to sell him. Do this and you'll have both his interest and his confidence. And if your product is capable of solving his problem or filling his need, you'll have a sale.

By now I'm sure you have a very natural question in mind. You want to know: "Will these interest-arousing techniques really work for me?" The only answer is: *some will and some won't.*

You are an unique individual. Therefore, some of these interest-arousing techniques will fit neither your product nor your personality. I, for example, would feel quite foolish using my friend Paul's method of drawing attention with carrots sticking out of my pockets. I'd feel quite uncomfortable using some of the thought-provoking headlines used in many advertising pieces. Yet I find that many of the other techniques we've discussed fit easily into my own sales presentations and are highly effective.

If you want to generate interest in your product, just select those techniques that fit your sales program and your sales personality. *And use them often.*

Enthusiasm is the great hill climber.
　　　　　　　　　　　　　　　— Elbert Hubbard

Psycho-Sales-Analysis Guide

*After reading Section 6, write
your answers to these questions:*

1. Do I know, or have I noted on my records, the major personal interest of each of my prospects and customers?

2. What can I do to help my prospects participate more actively in the sale?

3. What can I say or do on initial sales calls to make those sales calls:

    a. Appear more unusual?

    b. Appear more beneficial to the prospect?

4. What are three challenging questions I can use?

5. What are three shocking statements I can use?

6. What mechanical or visual devices can I use to add interest to my presentations?

7. Where can I obtain more testimonials for my product?

8. What are three things I can do to convince the prospect that I am sincerely interested in his welfare or needs?

9. How do I rate *(poor, fair,* or *excellent)* in these areas?

    a. Interesting presentations.

    b. Prospect participations.

c.   Use of sales aids.

d.   Belief in my product's value.

e.   Sincerity.

10.   What is the most important thing I can do to make my sales presentations more interesting?

Section 7

Psycho-Sales-Analysis Guide

*Before reading Section 7, write
your answers to these questions:*

1. What are the *exclusive* benefits of my product?

2. How do I present this information to my prospects?

3. Why should my prospects want to buy from my company instead of from competitive companies?

4. What factors make my product the best buy for the money?

5. What is my favorite method of demonstrating?

6. What demonstration methods are used by my competition?

7. Why is my demonstration method superior to the methods used by my competitors?

8. How do I show my prospects that my product is "easy to buy"?

9. How do I rate *(poor, fair,* or *excellent)* in these areas?

    a. Demonstrations.
    b. Proving product quality.
    c. Justifying product price.
    d. Selling against competition.
    e. Answering objections.

Making prospects want
your product

Now THAT you've found a legitimate prospect (one with both need and ability to buy), established contact with him, and generated interest, you're ready for the next step on The Golden Stairway to Successful Sales — creating preference for the specific brand product you sell.

Let's be sure that we understand the real difference between *interest* and *preference*.

A machine shop operator who has decided he wants a new lathe but hasn't decided *which* brand he should buy has interest but not preference. A man who wants to pave a parking lot at his factory but can't decide between asphalt and concrete has interest but not preference. The salesmen who implanted the idea of buying that new lathe or paving that parking lot are only part way toward their goal. These salesmen must now convince prospects that *their* lathe or *their* paving material offers the best and easiest solution to the prospect's need.

Reasons for indecision

What prevents a prospect from having a decided preference for your product? As a general rule there are four basic reasons why a prospect cannot bring himself to the point of wanting your product. In the back of his mind are these unanswered questions:

1. Is this the right product?
2. Is this the best price?
3. Are you the right source?
4. Is now the time to buy?

Because salesmen spend so much of their time selling it's sometimes difficult for them to analyze the thoughts of the man who is doing the buying. But salesmen are buyers, too. Remember the last time you went into a store to buy a suit? What thoughts went through your mind as you pawed through that rack of suits? Perhaps you said to yourself:

"I wonder if I'd look better in a tweed or a sharkskin weave?" (Is this the right product?)

"$125 is a lot of money to pay for this suit. Maybe I should look around and try to get a less expensive one." (Is this the best price?)

"This tweed looks good. I wonder if the store across the street has a better selection?" (Is this the right source?)

"They always have a clearance sale right after Christmas. Maybe I'd better wait." (Is now the time to buy?)

You may not have used these exact words but the chances are that you mentally covered several of these points while you were waiting for the salesman. Why? Because you, like all other human beings, are eager to get full value and satisfaction from every purchase you make.

How did the suit salesman help you answer those unvoiced questions in the back of your mind? Let's look at the well-organized and well-planned sales program he used to make you want to buy the suit.

After you mentioned color and size, the salesman probably said, "Let's try this coat on and check your size." He began his selling program by having you participate in the sale.

Also, he had taken your other coat and you couldn't very well walk out on him at this point. You were now a captive audience of one.

Next, the salesman positioned you in front of a mirror. Why? To let you see how the suit looked on you, to help you identify yourself with the product, and to let you visualize how it fulfilled your needs and desires. In short, this experienced salesman used a device (the mirror) so you could see the benefits of his merchandise with your own eyes. Then he began to talk about those benefits.

"It's a very nice fit, isn't it?" Anyone buying a suit should be interested in how the suit will fit.

"You seem to have lots of room in the shoulders." He assumes you are interested in buying a comfortable suit — isn't everyone?

"Notice the tight weave in this fabric; it will wear like iron." Most people are interested in long wear and service from the clothes they buy and you are probably no exception to this rule.

"How do you like this suit?" This is a key question to determine how you feel about this one particular suit. Does it meet your desires? The salesman is now probing. He wants to know how you feel about the suit before he tries to close the sale. This question also lets you participate in the sale, and voice any particular objections you may have.

The salesman finds your preference

If you said you didn't like the color or the fit, the salesman immediately put another coat on your back. He kept making changes until you finally agreed, with, "Yes, I think I like this suit"; or partially agreed, with, "It doesn't look too bad." Now the salesman knows you have a preference for the suit and he's ready to begin his close.

"If you'll just step into the dressing room we can see how the pants fit." At this point the salesman is testing to be sure you have a preference for this particular suit. If you go into the dressing room and try on the pants, he knows you're not only interested, but that you *want* the suit. By walking into the dressing room and trying on the pants you have indicated a preference and you're ready to be closed.

Here's the important point to remember: You walked into the clothing store in search of a suit. At that point you had *interest*. When the salesman finished his sales talk you had *preference* for one particular suit, a suit you had never seen before. Salesmanship (with your help) had changed interest into preference for the product the salesman was selling.

Suppose this salesman had failed to help you develop a decided preference for this one suit, or another one on his racks. Would you have bought from him? Certainly not! You'd have walked right out of that store and into another. Unless a salesman can change interest into a definite preference for a product, the sale cannot be made.

Demonstration – the key to creating preference

Regardless of the product or service being sold, the prospect likes to see and feel the merchandise. It's true that mail order customers cannot feel the merchandise before they buy, but they can see the merchandise by looking at the pictures in the catalog. A Sears, Wards, or Penney catalog without pictures would make very dull reading and do a poor job of selling.

Professional airplane salesmen create preference by taking their prospects on long, cross-country demonstration flights. They demonstrate the things the airplane will do for their prospects. They don't sell the airplane, they sell the airplane's *benefits*.

These airplane salesmen help their prospects experience the comfort and fun of flying; they take their prospects on business trips to prove that they can arrive at a destination relaxed, rested, and ready to conduct business.

If the airplane salesman does his job properly, the prospect will know (before he's asked to buy) that he needs the airplane in his business, that the salesman's brand of airplane will do more for him than other brands, and that the salesman can be trusted. Now the prospect has preference. Now he's ready to be closed.

Demonstrations take many forms

Airplanes or sweeping compound, the principle is the same. Sweeping compound salesmen also create desire for their product by demonstrating. They take their prospect into his factory, pour their brand of compound on the floor, and prove its "superior" benefits by actual demonstration. The prospect doesn't have to be told that this brand of sweeping compound is superior; he can see that it is with his own eyes.

The prospect can feel the absence of dust when he stoops down and runs his hand across the floor. If the compound is scented he can even smell its superior qualities. Will a demonstration of this type sell more sweeping compound than a mere sales talk? You can bet it will — every time!

Prospects for intangible products such as business insurance also like to "see and feel the merchandise." What they eventually buy is not a piece of paper called an insurance policy. What they buy is the protection the policy provides.

The successful business insurance salesman uses charts, graphs, and pictures to help his prospect visualize all the many security benefits his business will receive. The salesman creates preference for his policy by demonstrating its many *exclusive* benefits. He is able to create this preference by demonstrating with word pictures that enable the prospect to see the benefits he is being asked to buy.

Benefits which appeal to one prospect will not necessarily appeal to another. Take, for example, the problem of the automobile salesman. To create preference for his product he must talk different benefits to different types and classes of prospects.

For the town banker and his wife, the knowledgeable salesman presents a picture of prestige, economy, luxury, and comfort. But, when talking to a young drag-strip prospect, he must convert his thinking and his presentation to include the double-barreled carburetors, gear ratios, and mechanical gadgets with which his supersport models are equipped. The salesman must match product benefits with prospect interests.

A presentation must be interesting

The mark of an inexperienced salesman is his penchant for detailed and technical presentations of his product to prospects who have no interest in such features. When the salesman has finished his presentation, the prospect has no doubt that the salesman knows his product, but he's not certain what the product will do for him. He only knows how the product is put together and how it works.

Here's an important point that many salesmen (the unsuccessful ones) overlook: It's what interests the prospect that counts in a sale — not what interests the salesman. The salesman is not the one who will do the buying — the prospect is! This is why professionals in the selling field always tailor their presentations to the interests of the prospect rather than to their own interests.

If your ratio of sales to calls is not up to your expectations, ask yourself, "Am I impressing my prospects with my knowledge of my product? Or am I impressing them with all the things my product will do for them?"

The type of product you sell should determine the type of demonstration you give. If you are selling a mechanical device such as an automatic car washer, you can turn it on, let it run, and allow motion to hold the prospect's attention and gain his interest.

This demonstration technique was very effectively used by an airplane salesman friend of mine in Bremen, Germany.

The prospect had dropped by one morning just to see the facilities. He expressed an interest in an airplane which was not available for demonstration. However, there was another model in the hangar, and the salesman invited the prospect to take a demonstration flight which, because of the prospect's growing interest, lasted the whole day.

"It was getting dark," the salesman wrote in his letter to me, "and I had just about given up on the idea of closing the sale. Then I remembered your suggestion to 'turn it on and let it run.'

"I turned on all the lights; two landing lights, navigation lights, instrument panel lights, and the two rotating beacon lights. The prospect watched this 'Christmas tree' for a full ten minutes without saying a word. But I could almost see those flashing red lights reflecting in his eyes. Then he walked into the closing room where we opened a bottle of champagne and signed the order."

Four rules of demonstration

Professionals rely heavily on the demonstration to build product preference. They normally follow these four basic techniques regardless of the type of product or service being offered:

1. *Let the prospect see and feel the merchandise.* Everyone likes to see the product before he buys. Even when we buy through the mails, we do so only after seeing a picture of the product or building a mental picture from the description in the advertisement.

2. *Show the prospect how your product will solve his needs and fulfill his wants.* Did you ever buy a product without having a plan for its use? We all buy things with a definite reason in mind and these reasons are related to definite needs and wants that are personal to us.

3. *Show the prospect that he will get full value for his money.* Did you ever buy a product or service you knew was overpriced? Few people do.

4. *Show the prospect that your product is easy to buy.* "Only so many dollars a month" has become the watchword of our modern day economic order. Unless a product can be purchased without placing a financial strain on the buyer, it will probably not be bought. This is why financing and leasing programs have become such an important sales aid in the industrial sales field.

Handling the competition

The beginning salesman who sees sales lost to competition is apt to damn its existence. "If," he thinks, "I didn't have competition, I'd be able to sell more of my products."

Professional salesmen, however, take an entirely different view of competition. They recognize the fact that competition can be helpful to a salesman. It's competition that keeps us from getting fat and lazy; makes us research the products we sell to see where and how they are better than competitive products; and helps us sharpen our selling skills. Without competition the fun in selling would be gone, the challenge would disappear, and there would be no need for salesmen. Prospects would beat a path to the product maker's door and demand the product.

If the product you sell has value, other salesmen will see that it has and competition will always result. The first ballpoint pens sold for $25 and the demand was tremendous. Company after company jumped on the bandwagon of this profitable new item.

Today you can buy a good ballpoint pen for 25¢ instead of $25 and the selling cream has been skimmed from the top. Yet there are many *professional* salesmen who still make excellent incomes from the quantity sale of ballpoint pens to industry and wholesale-retail outlets.

Since competition is a constant factor in the sales field, the professional salesman has learned to follow two basic "don'ts" and one basic "do" when facing up to his competition.

Two basic "don'ts"

Don't mention competition unless your prospect does. Every time you mention your competition by name, you're advertising for him. Constant reference to your competition can create only one thought in your prospect's mind: "Perhaps I'd better take a look at the competitive product."

It's possible that your prospect has no real interest in the competitive product. He may not even be aware of its existence. If you bring up the subject, you're placing a hurdle in your own path. So, let the competition advertise and sell their own wares. You concentrate on selling yours.

Don't try to unsell competition. It's a very natural impulse to want to knock a competitive product, to run it down, and to prove what *you* know (that is, their product is not nearly as good as yours). But hold off on that impulse. The moment you start to "talk down" the competition, your prospect will tend to discount almost everything you say. Why? Because the prospect considers you an expert on your product only. He won't believe that you know all about the competitive product. Besides, you're only challenging him to find out if the things you're saying about the competitive product are true. The more you talk about the competition, the more your prospect will want to investigate.

I'm sure you've had the experience of walking into a store and asking for a brand product that wasn't available at that store. The salesman tried to sell you his brand by claiming that the asked-for brand was of poor quality, wouldn't wear well, or was overpriced. He didn't bother to tell you what was good about his own brand — he only told you what was bad about the competitive brand.

Did you buy? Probably not. Your reaction was understandably negative.

The salesman who spends his time talking down the competition instead of building up the benefits of his own product is simply feeding orders to his competitors.

One basic "do"

Do recognize competition and sell professionally. When competition enters the picture, the professional salesman doesn't bury his head in the sand. Instead, he acknowledges that competition does exist (the prospect knows this), and that the competitive product does have *some* good features and benefits (the prospect suspects this). And then he turns the prospect's attention back to his own product.

The professional says, "I really don't know all the facts about Brand X, Mr. Prospect, but I do know that my product has these *exclusive* benefits which are very important to you," and then commences to enumerate them. By doing this, the salesman has acknowledged the competition without damning or praising it, supplied an answer to his prospect's questions about competition, and put the subject back on the track to his own product.

Note that the old pro hasn't said the competitive product lacks certain features or benefits. He's only said that *his* product has certain *exclusive* benefits.

Sometimes salesmen are forced into the corner of comparison. The prospect insists that a comparison be made between the salesman's product and the competitor's product. When this happens, the professional uses a "third party" device. Instead of trying to be an authority on the comparison, he will refer to comparison charts, articles favorable to his product, or other authoritative and printed information:

"Let's see what my technical handbook says about the competitive product, Mr. Prospect." Or, "The *Rock Quarry*

Gazette had an interesting article comparing these products, Mr. Prospect. Let's see how they feel about the relative merits of the two."

Using printed literature to answer questions about the competition has great psychological impact. All through our school years we were taught to believe in the printed word. If the textbook presented a statement as a fact, it was seldom, if ever, questioned. This habit stays with most of us, and if we read it in the newspaper or see it in a magazine we're likely to accept the statement as "gospel truth." The wise salesman, knowing this fact, arms himself with every bit of printed support he can manage to find.

Now that you're on sound footing on Step 4 — you've made your prospect want your product — it's time to move on. Your prospect now believes that: (1) your product is the right product, and (2) you are the right source.

Your next challenge is to convince the prospect that: (3) your price is right, and (4) now is the time to buy.

How can you find out if the price is right and the time to buy has arrived? That's easy, you simply ask for the order, which is the next step (Step 5) on The Golden Stairway to Successful Sales.

The only way to make money is to render a service for humanity — to supply something that people want — and to carry things from where they are plentiful to where they are needed.

— Elbert Hubbard

Psycho-Sales-Analysis Guide

*After reading Section 7, write
your answers to these questions:*

1. What can I do or say to convince my prospect that:

    a. My product is the best one for his needs?

    b. I am the right source for that product?

    c. My price is right?

    d. Today is the day he should buy?

2. How can I vary my demonstration to appeal to the different interests of different prospects?

3. What specific answers can I give my prospects if they raise objections to:

    a. My product's quality?

    b. My product's price?

    c. My product's performance?

4. What are the specific benefits my prospects will receive by dealing with me? With my company?

5. What should I do when my prospects or customers:

    a. Mention my competition by name?

    b. Insist on a comparison of my product and competitive products?

Section 8

Psycho-Sales-Analysis Guide

*Before reading Section 8, write
your answers to these questions:*

1. Remembering a recent successful sale, how did I know it was time to ask for the order? (The prospect's actions, statements, questions, etc.)

2. What's the worst thing that can happen to me if I ask for the order and the customer says no?

3. What are the reasons other salesmen I know sometimes fail to ask for the order?

4. What are the exact words I used the last time I asked for an order?

5. What words do I use most when I ask for an order?

6. Have I ever sold my product when I did not, in some way, ask for the order?

7. How do I rate *(poor, fair,* or *excellent)* in these areas?

   a. Aggressiveness.

   b. Leadership.

   c. Clarity of thought.

   d. Alertness.

   e. Initiative.

How to ask for the order

You're now nearing the top of The Golden Stairway to Successful Sales. You've researched and completed Step 1 to find a prospect who has the need and ability to buy your product. You've established contact with the prospect (Step 2), aroused his interest (Step 3), and created preference for your product (Step 4). At this point in the sales effort, your prospect, in addition to having both the need for your product and the ability to buy it, should also have the desire to buy. The basic requirements of need, ability, and desire have now been established. The sale can now be completed *if* you take the next step on The Golden Stairway — asking for the order.

This is the sales step which separates the men from the boys. Every sales manager who has ever lived has seen salesmen with outstanding ability in finding and preselling prospects but who "freeze" at the simple task of asking for the order. These sales managers have known countless salesmen who could make flawless demonstrations but could not bring themselves to the point of asking for the order. Like the quarterback who leads his team the length of the football field only to be stopped on the one-yard line, the salesman who cannot ask for the order can never be a star.

Herein lies the magic of The Golden Stairway in selling. If all the groundwork has been properly laid (Steps 1 through 4 completed), the prospect finds himself in this frame of mind: He is now interested in your product. He now wants your product. He knows you are a salesman. He expects you to ask for the order, and he probably won't buy unless you do just that — ask for the order!

Are you sure a prospect won't buy unless you ask for the order? I am. I learned this lesson many years ago when I was selling office duplicating machines. The prospect, his wife (who was also his partner in the business), and I were sitting in their small office. We'd reviewed all the benefits my duplicator would give them and I'd run out of things to say. Silence reigned. Finally the wife stood up, looked me straight in the eye, and said, "Young man, is there something about this machine you haven't told us? You haven't asked us to sign an order. Is there some reason why we shouldn't?"

Asking for the order can lead to only one of two prospect actions:

- The prospect can say yes and the sale can be closed.

- The prospect can say no and open up a whole new course of action for the salesman. Now the salesman can concentrate on finding out exactly *why* the prospect said no.

It has been said that a real salesman begins to sell when the prospect says no. A simple no is a challenge to be met. Until this moment, the sale has been like many other sales which preceded it; but now it's to become more interesting and more exciting. Now the professional selling man can really go to work and prove his professionalism!

As a general rule you'll discover that three elementary reasons lie behind a prospect's "no" answer to a request for the order:

1. *The basic selling steps haven't been completed.* Imagine yourself as a computer salesman who, after many carefully conducted presentations and demonstrations, has asked a farm equipment manufacturer to buy a computer. The manufacturer says no. Now what can you do?

Perhaps your prospect has no real interest in updating and modernizing his plant. Before you can sell him your computer you'll have to rework Step 3 — sparking prospect interest.

Perhaps your prospect has been talking with another computer salesman and feels that Brand X may be more suited to his needs. What can you do? You can go back and rework Step 4 — making the prospect want your product.

How can you find out if the prospect has no real interest in modernizing his plant or does have an interest in Brand X? That's not hard to do. You just ask.

Professional salesmen know that they must ask for the order before the prospect is likely to say yes, no, or maybe. A "no" response to the question "Will you buy?" can always be followed with another question, "Why?" The answer the prospect gives to this "why" counter-question will usually indicate that you've failed to complete one or more of the basic sales steps.

2. *Centers of influence may be blocking the sale.* No man is an island unto himself. All of us are surrounded by people whose opinions we respect and whose displeasures we fear. A man whose wife nags and complains about the time he spends fishing will hesitate to buy a boat. A corporate treasurer trying to conserve his company's assets may deter the president from adding to plant facilities. Business associates who love to joke can make a manager fearful of purchasing a prestige product.

Even though a man may really want your product his centers of influence (the people who exercise an invisible power over his decisions) may make him hesitate to buy.

Professional salesmen always probe for information about centers of influence when the prospect should buy but won't, and the real reason for this refusal is unknown to the salesman.

The power which centers of influence hold was vividly demonstrated not long ago by the problem of an airplane salesman friend of mine. Two different prospects signed orders for airplanes and gave this salesman substantial deposit checks only to stop payment on them and cancel their orders.

After the salesman was blocked in all efforts to talk personally with his former customers, he used a third-party device to discover these facts: The first man's wife objected to his flying. The second man's company treasurer felt the purchase was ill-timed and that this action would deplete the company's too-low cash reserves.

Armed with this new information, the salesman began a revitalized sales campaign directed towards these influence centers. He was finally able to invite the first man *and his wife* to an out-of-town Sunday luncheon and, of course, they flew in the airplane he wanted to sell. "I had no idea these little airplanes had so many instruments in them," the wife commented. "Why, these little airplanes can go anywhere the big airplanes can, can't they!"

The first man bought his airplane!

A visit by the salesman to the second man's company treasurer brought equally happy results. When the salesman explained that the airplane could be leased with an option to buy, and that modest monthly payments would protect the company's cash reserves, the treasurer withdrew his objection to the sale.

The second man also bought (leased) his airplane!

An unusual story? Not at all. The professionals realize that they often have to sell just as hard to people who surround the buyer as they do to the buyer himself.

3. *Your prospect has to justify his purchase.* Sometimes even the most experienced of salesmen forget that purchasing agents, managers, department heads, and other company buyers are human beings, too. These people are influenced by the same psychological motivators which influence the salesman when he buys things for himself and his family. Perhaps the best way for a salesman to understand his prospects is to understand himself and how he (the salesman) is influenced to buy or not to buy a product.

Justifying a purchase

Think back to the moment when you bought your present car. This was a large family expenditure, and as such, required considerable justification. I'm guessing that some thoughts like these went through your mind. They began as you were watching an exciting television commercial. A beautiful new auto was pictured on the screen, and an announcer described it in dulcet tones. Your interest was aroused, and naturally, that weekend, you went to the display room "just to take a look."

You began to develop certain symptoms of "new car fever" the moment you walked through the dealer's door. A salesman greeted you, but you managed to fend him off, saying you wanted time to think about it.

As you drove home, psychology went to work. The engine of your old car appeared to develop a knock. It didn't seem to have much pickup. The brakes didn't hold too well, either. And there was that squeak again! In short, you were bitten by the "new car bug."

So, you persuaded yourself that you *needed* that new car. Thanks to extended time payments, you felt you could *afford* it. Since the car you were driving was practically a jalopy by now, there was no question you *wanted* a new model. Need, ability to buy, and desire: the three elements for the sale were there. But still you didn't *buy*. Why? The answer is simple. You had to justify that purchase to yourself — and probably to your wife as well.

Chances are that you, like most other members of the human race on occasion, used one or more of seven psychological motivators which move people to buy. One or more of these basic motivators probably helped you justify your desire for that new car:

1) *Love of family.* A man willingly spends money for children's swing sets, mink stoles, and countless other things he himself will never use or enjoy.

2) *Pride.* How many. of us live in houses we really can't afford?

3) *Prestige.* Have you ever joined a club or social group just to enhance your standing among your friends or business associates? Most people have.

4) *Desire to lead.* Have you ever volunteered your services in a church group, club, or civic organization? Do you recall the good feeling this action gave you?

5) *Desire for new things.* Check your newspaper. See how many times the word "new" appears in advertising headlines. It *is* fun to be the first in your neighborhood or business to own a brand new product, isn't it?

6) *Progress.* The emphasis being placed today on education reflects every man's dream of making progress in life.

7) *Profit.* This is why we have savings accounts, buy stocks and bonds, and work in our business, trade, or profession.

Now then, let's get back to that new car you wanted to buy. You and your wife sat down to talk over the idea of owning a new car. Did you use psychological justification on yourself? I'm betting you did and that your conversation with your wife included statements such as these:

"Mary Jane is driving now and those brakes on the old car could go out any time." (Love of family.)

"The neighbors can afford a new car so I guess we can too." (Pride.)

I don't know who first said this but it's certainly true: Isn't it amazing how we'll go into debt just to buy things we don't need to impress people we can't stand the sight of!

"We're driving the oldest car on the block, and besides, you've got to look successful if you're going to be successful." (Prestige.)

Or you may have said:

"The repair bills on the old bus are eating us out of house and home." (Profit.)

Now then, what have you done to yourself? In your own mind you've conjured up a mixture of psychological and economic *excuses* to help justify the purchase of a new car. Excuses? Sure they are. Just look at that statement about "repair bills on the old bus are eating us out of house and home."

You know it's true and I know it's true that for less than $200 you could probably put that old car into A-1 shape and drive it a year or even two years more. It will cost you at least $2,000 (that's 10 times as much) to buy the new car.

You could borrow the $200 for repairs and pay off the loan at $10 per month. But instead of doing this, you're talking yourself into buying a new car, and borrowing $2,000 which you'll have to pay off at the rate of $100 per month.

Is this decision economically sound? You know it isn't. But, because you want a new car so badly, you're willing to build up mental justification for your action.

Remember your own mental gymnastics when you have a prospect who really wants your product. When you ask for the order and he says, "I'd really like to buy your product, but . . . ," remember that he's pleading with you to help him justify his desire. Successful salesmen are the ones who are willing to do just that — they help the prospect justify his actions. Successful salesmen are always willing to help the prospect prove to himself that: (1) he's a wise businessman; (2) buying the product is a decision that's economically sound; and (3) the benefits the product offers are really worth the money that must be spent to get them.

Find the barrier to your sale

Now let's be pragmatic. We're salesmen but we're not mind readers. Our prospects, hung on a psychological fence, are probably not going to tell us the real reason they won't buy. Would you admit to a salesman that your wife won't let you use household account money to buy things for the business? Would you explain to a salesman that your partner, not you, has the final say when it comes to spending your company's money? Certainly not!

Knowing this, the professional salesman begins to probe. "You say you want my product, Mr. Prospect, yet you appear to be uncomfortable about buying it today. Why?"

Many times this question, or one like it, will bring about an evasive or noncommittal answer. So the salesman begins to talk benefits. He supplies answers to questions he thinks may be in the back of the prospect's mind. He'll ask questions such as, "How does your partner feel about expanding your production with this machine?" Or he may say, "Doesn't Mr. Jones in accounting agree this machine will reduce his overtime expenditures?"

The selling professional knows that if you have the need, the ability to buy, and the desire for the product, and still won't buy, you need to justify the purchase to someone. He then attempts to find and identify that barrier. Once this is done the salesman can supply the justification the prospect is seeking.

A verbal request that the prospect buy your product is the most common method of asking for the order. Many professionals, however, have found that a written proposal is often a more effective way of getting the prospect to say yes. This is particularly true if the cost of the product or service is high, or if the selling has taken place over a long period of time.

A written request for the order can be as simple as a set of notes on the back of a price list. Or it can be as complex as a documentary presentation detailing a truck-leasing program for a large transportation corporation. While the format and length of the proposal will vary, almost all well-written proposals have these elements in common (and please note the prospect's reaction to the written request for the order):

The case for a written proposal

1.   *A proposal creates interest.* "There's my name and my company's name on that piece of paper. This is written about my needs. Maybe this paper will tell me what the product will do for me and my company."

2.   *A proposal challenges.* "Is all this really true? Does this salesman have the correct facts about my company and my company's needs?"

3.   *A proposal defines and states the prospect's need.* "Is this really the product we need? Will it actually solve our problems?"

4.   *A proposal shows how the product answers the need.* "So this is how the product is going to solve the problem we talked about."

5.   *A proposal shows the prospect an easy and acceptable way to buy.* "I never realized it before but I can buy all this for only $5 a week. And that's less than I spend on cigars."

Written proposals offer many advantages over the more commonly used verbal request for the order. A written proposal establishes a dignified business climate. Now there can be no misunderstanding between the salesman and the prospect. Everything is down in black and white.

Using a written proposal helps the salesman organize his presentation in step-by-step fashion. He can proceed from one point to the next, outline specific benefits in order of importance, and be sure that each and every important sales point has been thoroughly covered. Last, and most important, a written proposal eliminates unnecessary discussion and focuses attention on the salesman's goal — the closing of the sale.

Quite frequently a written proposal will help you uncover hidden objections. Up to this point your prospect has not had to explain to you why he is or is not interested in your product. Put a written proposal in front of him and you force the issue in a dignified way. You have taken the time and made the effort to write down all the reasons why he should buy. Now he, in turn, should feel an obligation to explain any reason why he is not willing to buy.

How should you ask for the order?

While conducting sales seminars I frequently ask each of the participating salesmen to explain the exact words and actions he uses when asking for the prospect's order. Most of the time these salesmen are selling the same or similar products. But I have yet to encounter two salesmen in any group (and this includes groups as large as 40 or more) who use exactly the same words and actions to ask for the order.

The reasons for the many variations in method are obvious. No two salesmen have the same personality. No two prospects are exactly alike. Different products, different prospects, different needs and desires, plus a million or so other differences make it impossible to establish a best method of asking for the order.

There is, however, one point of commonality in all successful requests for the order. The prospect has no doubt that the salesman is sincere and is asking him to sign that order — today — at this very moment.

Few girls ever misunderstand a proposal of marriage. You can say "let's get married" on the very first date. Or you can use a full year's program of flowers and music before you pop the question. Regardless of how you say it, or how long it took you to get around to saying it, she'll understand you if you're really serious.

Still have qualms about asking for the order? Think of it this way. Prospects with the need, ability to buy, and desire for your product are no more insulted or annoyed by your request for their order than a girl is when she is asked for her hand in marriage. When wooing girls or prospects, you have to ask the question if you want to reach your goal.

Asking for the order sets the stage for the next step on The Golden Stairway — closing the sale. But first let's answer the following questions and see if we can't improve our technique of asking for the order.

This habit of expectancy always marks the strong man. It is a form of attraction; our own comes to us because we desire it. We find what we expect to find, and we receive what we ask for.

— Elbert Hubbard

Psycho-Sales-Analysis Guide

*After reading Section 8, write
your answers to these questions:*

1. How can I make my request for the order more positive and therefore more effective?

2. What centers of influence are most likely to interfere with the sale of my product or service?

3. What objections can be expected from these centers of influence and how will I answer these objections?

4. Which of the psychological motivators can I use to make the prospect want my product?

5. What can I say or do to help my prospects justify the purchase of my product? List their objections and their justifications.

    a. To themselves.

    b. To other people (centers of influence).

6. If I used a written proposal to ask for the order, what would be the advantages and the disadvantages?

7. Would the use of a written proposal help me make more sales or fewer sales? Explain fully.

Section 9

Psycho-Sales-Analysis Guide

*Before reading Section 9, write
your answers to these questions:*

1. Do my customers buy for *emotional* or *logical* reasons?
   List some of their reasons.

2. Recall a recent successful sale in which an objection
   was raised. What was the objection and how did I
   answer it?

3. Remember a recent "unsuccessful sale" in which an
   objection was raised.

   a. What was the prospect's objection?

   b. How did I try to handle it?

   c. What might I have done to save the sale?

4. When a prospect says the price is too high, what do I
   normally say and do?

5. When a prospect says my product's quality is poor,
   what do I normally say or do?

6. How do I rate myself *(poor, fair,* or *excellent)* in the
   following areas?

   a. Courage.

   b. Argument avoidance.

   c. Poise under stress.

   d. Tact and diplomacy.

124

Closing the sale

Now THAT you've located the prospect, contacted him, aroused his interest, created a strong desire for your product, and asked him to buy — all that remains to be done is to close the sale.

If all the previous sales steps have been properly completed there's really no *logical* reason for the prospect to refuse to buy. Yet sometimes mere logic will not suffice. The prospect needs to become excited about his pending purchase. He has to get a bit emotional. You, as the salesman, must be prepared to help him become emotional.

Let's talk about the role that logic and emotion play in the closing of a sale. Both are usually involved but in different degrees depending on the product or service being offered.

How emotion and logic are involved in the close

The extent to which emotion and logic are involved in the closing effort will depend, in a large measure, on the price of the product being sold. To illustrate this point let's consider the president of a large corporation.

Emotional factors might induce the president to buy a new $200 adding machine for his secretary. But it would take considerable logic to induce this same man to buy a $2 million electronic computer for his plant. Thus, the higher the price of the product, the more need there is for logic, and for justification with facts instead of opinions.

The president of our hypothetical corporation *might* have to justify the purchase of the $200 adding machine to his wife (especially if she knew the secretary was to benefit from the purchase). The president probably *would* have to justify the purchase of the $2 million computer to his stockholders, or at least to his board of directors.

Knowing these facts, a professional adding machine salesman would talk about his machine making life easier for the secretary while making her more efficient. The computer salesman, however, would have to use factual case histories to show how his equipment had reduced expensive overtime in other plants, increased the efficiency of their operations, and (ideally) how the computer had paid for itself in a specified period of time.

The adding machine salesman could use opinions with an emotional presentation. The computer salesman would be far more successful if he used facts in a logic-keyed presentation.

Does this mean that emotion and logic apply only to corporation presidents? Not at all! The average man has much in common with our corporation president. You and I may get very emotional about a $1.98 fishing lure. Yet it's going to take logic (and lots of it) to make us part with $198.98 for a course in salesmanship.

Handling objections during the close

If the salesman has done a professional selling job, most of the prospect's objections will have been answered early in the sale and before the close is attempted. Quite often, however, the prospect will hide his objections until he's forced into that decision-making corner of the closing room.

When objections are raised during the close, a professional

salesman attempts to dispense with them as quickly as possible. Why? Because he's there to close, not to debate. So the salesman tries to be brief and factual. He avoids lengthy discussions. His objective is to keep moving toward the close and to get the prospect to say "yes" instead of "but."

Stalling for time

Sometimes a prospect will raise an objection merely to stall the moment of final decision. He may not be certain in his own mind that now is the time to buy and he wants to gain time to think about his decision. Frequently, his objection will be voiced in the form of a question having little or no relevance, such as "What weight metal is used to make your product?" Then, while you're deeply involved in answering this unimportant question, the prospect will be thinking up excuses for not buying your product. He's using an offensive tactic as a defense against being closed.

Does the question asked by the prospect during a close show that a real objection exists? Or is the question merely a stall for time? When the salesman answers these questions in his own mind, he's ready to handle the question.

If the salesman believes that the objection being raised is legitimate, he answers it. If he feels the objection is being raised as a distraction, he tries to sidestep the objection and keep moving toward the close.

"Is this question really important to you, Mr. Prospect? If it is I can get an answer for you. Meanwhile, let's consider these exclusive benefits my product will provide for you."

Use specific words — ask specific questions

If the salesman has done his homework properly, he knows, long before attempting to close, the product which exactly fits his prospect's needs. He has concentrated the prospect's attention on that specific product. He doesn't try to close the sale of bottling machinery. He tries to close the sale of the Model K12, Green and Gray, Automatic Bottle Capper, Serial Number Z4876298 (that's the machine now stored in the local warehouse and available for immediate delivery).

The salesman doesn't ask, "Isn't green and gray *about* the color you want, Mr. Prospect?" If he does, the prospect can readily agree that the colors are "about" what he wants without committing himself. Use indefinite words — about, almost, approximately — and you'll go around in circles all day without getting a commitment from the prospect.

The professional salesman is specific. He asks, "Isn't green and gray the exact color combination you want for your Kansas City plant, Mr. Prospect?" If the prospect says yes to this question, he's hooked. The color question is settled once and for all time. The prospect is one step down the road toward the signing of the contract.

Suppose the prospect answers no to the color question. There's no harm done. Now the salesman can say, "Oh — then what colors *do* you prefer on *your* machine? Fine. We can order those exact colors for you. Now you did want the deluxe bottle counter and variable speed control on *your* bottle capper, right?"

Examine the prospect's objections

Now the salesman, by using specific words, making definite statements, and asking exact questions, is uncovering and answering any final objections the prospect may have. His objective in these tactics? The salesman is making the prospect lay all of his objections out on the table where they can be examined and handled deftly, quickly, and finally. Sooner or later the prospect will run out of objections. When this happens the prospect has no alternative but to sign the order.

Listen to professional selling men at work. You'll never hear them say, "You *should* like this model, Mr. Prospect."

Instead, you'll hear them say, "You'll like this Model K12, Mr. Prospect, because it has the fast bottling speed you need for extra profits, the colors that fit your plant, and the variable speed control you said you wanted." Once a prospect has agreed to such a positive statement (or failed to refute it immediately) he's almost obligated to buy.

Be sure you understand your prospect's desires

Many sales have been lost simply because the salesman did not fully understand the prospect's real needs and desires. Let me tell you about an almost-lost sale which illustrates this point.

An Oklahoma airplane salesman met a walk-in prospect who volunteered the information that he was "looking for an airplane which could carry five people, fly 1,200 miles non-stop, and fly at speeds of about 200 miles per hour."

"Fine," said the salesman. "I have just the airplane you're looking for," and he gave the prospect a demonstration flight in a $60,000 model.

After the flight, the prospect appeared to be unimpressed. "I don't think I'm interested in this airplane," he told the salesman.

"Why not?" the salesman asked. "I've just shown you the exact airplane you described. It carries five passengers, has a 1,250 mile range, and flies at 212 miles per hour."

"But this airplane is for my wife's mother," explained the prospect. "She's the one who's paying for it. We take her to Phoenix every winter. But she's crippled and I don't think she can climb up on the wing and get in and out of this airplane very easily."

So the salesman demonstrated again, this time in a larger airplane with a stairway that extended to the ground when the door was opened — and closed a $178,500 sale!

What a man says and what he means may be two entirely different things. So, before attempting to close a sale, the professional salesman makes sure he understands the exact needs and desires of his prospect.

Overselling can lose the sale

In every good salesman there's a bit of the actor who likes to be "on stage." If we didn't like to be at the center of things, to command attention, and to evoke emotions from our prospects, we'd have selected a more sedentary profession. But sometimes we can talk too much. There's a time for talk, and there's a time for silence, too.

It's at the close of the sale that the temptation to talk is the strongest. We've worked hard to reach this moment of decision. We may even be a bit nervous because so much is at stake. So we tense up. We talk more than we should. We talk so much and speak so loudly that the poor prospect is not only prevented from participating in the sale — he's also prevented from thinking. And when a prospect can't think, he's understandably reluctant to make that all-important decision to buy.

When the presentation is made and you've asked for the order, give your prospect a moment to collect his thoughts. You're pressing for a decision. You need to apply pressure. So, remember this very important fact about selling: *Silence can be the strongest possible pressure you can apply in a closing situation.*

Stand back. Fold your arms. Look directly at the prospect, and let (or make) him speak first. You'll be surprised at the number of times he'll say yes just to relieve the pressure that your silence brings.

And *please*, when you do get the order, thank your customer and leave. Do this as quickly and gracefully as you can. Your business there is completed. Don't continue selling. This customer could think of something new in the way of an objection and want to rethink his decision. You could sell yourself out of the sale. It's happened before, many times, and it can always happen again. It could happen to *you!*

One basic rule of selling should be mentioned before price quoting is discussed. You should never try to up-grade a prospect beyond his ability to buy.

Professional salesmen understand this basic rule. They also understand, however, that they get bigger commission checks when they work on the high side of the prospect's pocketbook. Show the prospect your deluxe model first. If it's beyond his ability to buy, he'll probably let you know. And it's easier to come down in price than it is to go up in price. A friend of mine in power transmission equipment sales expresses the thought this way: "If you don't show your $137,000 generator, you haven't got much chance of selling your $137,000 generator." So he always starts talking at the top of his line.

The art of quoting price

Quite often the price, if lower than the competition's, will be a benefit which should be mentioned time and time again throughout the sales presentation. But on "high ticket" items, such as computerized milling machines and locomotives, the price is more of a barrier than a benefit. In such cases, the professional selling man knows he must use finesse when quoting price. How? He attempts to depreciate the price by making the benefits of his product loom so large in the prospect's mind that price ceases to be a factor.

If the price is a frequently mentioned objection to the product you sell, your prospect himself will bring up the subject. Let him. Try to work in as many benefits as you can *before* the question of price is mentioned. Why? Because you'll be talking about all the reasons why the prospect *should* buy rather than the one reason why he *should not.*

When working with high priced merchandise, most professionals try to talk price only twice in their sales presentations: once when the prospect mentions the subject, and once during the closing attempt.

"I probably can't afford this item," the prospect is saying to himself the first time he asks about price. If his suspicions are confirmed at this point by the blunt quote of a high price, the sale is probably lost. This is why the professional salesman attempts to slide over the price the first time it's mentioned.

The experienced salesman says, "This four-color printing press you're looking at, Mr. Prospect, lists out at $386,975 *but this price includes* extra inking rollers, optional sheet counters, a five-year extended warranty contract, and full insurance coverage plus many other options you may not want right now."

Now let's look at what has happened. As the salesman runs down the long list of optional and extra-cost items, he'll mention some items the prospect will not want on his machine. So, as the salesman is talking, the prospect is thinking, "I can buy this printing press for less than the $386,975 quoted because I really don't need all those optional items." The prospect now has an escape. He can delay the moment of decision. He can afford to expose himself a little longer. The quotation of a high price hasn't scared him away.

The right time to quote price

Suppose the salesman had simply answered the price question by saying, "This printing press costs $386,975," and then stopped talking. The prospect would automatically have a negative reaction. "Too much money," he'd probably say to himself. The door to the sale would have been slammed shut by the blunt quotation of a price.

What if the prospect continues to raise the price question before the salesman is ready to close? One stock answer has served knowledgeable salesmen for many years: "It all depends on how you want *your* press equipped, Mr. Prospect. Now let me show you . . . ." Then the salesman quickly swings back into his presentation of benefits until they become more important than price to the prospect.

After the salesman is certain the prospect does have a genuine desire for the product and is ready to be closed, the price can be quoted safely. This time the salesman quotes directly from the order form, details the price of each optional equipment item, and confidently announces the total price.

Shaving the price can cut your throat

In an era which has seen the rise of the discount house, many prospects are hesitant to pay the quoted price for a product. Many purchasing agents prefer to ignore the published price list and invariably ask the salesman for an expected discount. The result is that many of today's salesmen have become price negotiators.

The man who is a selling professional understands the economics of the price-cutting game. He knows that every bit of a price cut must be subtracted from the profit in a sale, and that profits must be made to stay in business. Just look at what happens to a salesman who works on a 20%-from-list-price margin if he cuts the price by 10%:

	Full price	10% discount
Unit selling price. . . . . . .$	100	$ 90
Unit cost to seller	80	80
Profit per unit	20	10
Number of units sold	x 1	x 2
Balanced profit . . . .$	20	$ 20

This salesman needs 100% more unit volume to recover his lost profit. He must now sell two units instead of one. He must increase the dollar volume of his sales from $100 to $180, and that's an 80% increase *just to break even.* Furthermore, these figures fail to consider the added cost of stocking and handling the extra unit that must be sold to retain the $20 profit. If he cuts the price by 15%:

	Full price	15% discount
Unit selling price.	.$100	$85
Unit cost to seller	80	80
Profit per unit	20	5
Number of units sold	x 1	x 4
Balanced profit	.$ 20	$ 20

Now the salesman needs 400% more unit volume to recoup lost profits. Instead of one unit he must now sell four. Where he previously sold $100 worth of merchandise he must now sell $340 worth. His unit costs will rise because of increased stocking and handling expenses. This salesman is in real trouble.

There's no skill involved in cutting price. Anyone can do it. The skill in selling comes from building benefits in the buyer's mind until product benefits tower far above the price barrier. Thus, the professional selling man is always ready for the price buyer, but he's not ready to cut his price.

Six things to do before reducing the price

Most salesmen rank the question of price next to closing as the most difficult facet of selling. What can you do when the prospect tells you he can buy the same product or service somewhere else for less money?

For many years the professional salesman has used six basic rules for handling this situation:

1. *Don't panic.* You know the product you sell is worth the price you're asking or you wouldn't be selling it. Stand

firm. Be confident in your belief in price value and you'll be dealing from a position of psychological strength.

2. *Get all the facts.* Can this prospect really buy somewhere else for less money? Or is he just bluffing? Find out the true answers to these two questions. Many prices have been lowered unnecessarily because of a mistaken belief that the prospect could buy elsewhere for less money. Find out *why* the competition's price is lower.

3. *Reason with your prospect.* Don't debate or argue the price question. There's usually a difference in price when values are different. Lower quality products can always be sold at a lower price. So demonstrate or redemonstrate the values that are in the product or service you're selling. Ask your prospect to be reasonable, too. Ask him to agree that your product's *exclusive* benefits justify the higher price it commands on the market.

One very effective technique in dealing with businessmen price buyers is to ask if they give discounts on the products they manufacture or sell. "What do you do when one of your customers asks you to cut your price, Mr. Prospect? You have to make a fair profit to stay in business, don't you?" If your prospect is a reasonable man, such logic will help you defend *and get* the price you've asked.

4. *Sell your company, too.* Your company is different than any other company in the world. Does it offer faster service than the competition? Does it have better warranty policies? Is your company's reputation for fair dealing well known? Stress these and other exclusive benefits the prospect will gain by trading with your company. Be sure he understands that these benefits are included in the price you're asking for your product.

5. *Cite the dangers of price buying.* Anyone can make a product and sell it cheaply *if* he leaves out quality. We've all had one or more sad experiences when we bought because of the price tag. You don't have to mention the competition by

name when you tell your prospect about others who bought because of a lower price and lived to regret their decision. Poor quality is never a bargain and your prospect is aware of this fact of business life. Just remind him that you're asking a higher price for higher quality.

6. *Weigh the value of price reduction.* If you do cut your price today, are you setting a dangerous precedent? Will you be required to cut your price again with the next prospect? The long-range benefits of holding a price line may make it advisable for you to pass up a particular sale. No professional salesman is interested in giving his product away. The whole object of selling is to make a fair profit.

Not long ago, while attending a construction equipment trade show in Chicago, Illinois, I overheard a conversation between a salesman and a prospect. They were dickering over the price of a giant earth-moving machine. "Dammit, Joe," the prospect said to the salesman, "I'm not asking you for mercy, *but I do expect justice.*"

These words, I believe, describe the fear in every prospect's heart when the question of price is raised. Every customer wants to be sure the price he pays for the product is no more than the price the next man will have to pay.

Your prospect wants to be an astute businessman. He's willing to pay the going rate for your product, but he's not willing to pay more. He isn't necessarily asking for special consideration. He's testing — and he's asking for fair play.

The salesman who convinces his prospect that the price being quoted is the lowest possible price, that the next customer will not buy the product for less, is the salesman who gets both the order *and* the price he asks.

How to handle the price buyer

Every salesman meets him sooner or later: the man whose only interest seems to be in getting a bargain. Benefits, quality, and exclusive features all seem secondary in this prospect's mind. His thoughts are focused on price, price, price! He is "out to get a real deal."

What can you do about this type of individual? Professional salesmen have a very easy and effective way of handling the price buyer. The salesman quotes his best price — his final price and the one which will still produce a reasonable profit. The salesman quotes the price just once. If the bargain hunter accepts, well and good. A sale is made. If the bargain hunter doesn't buy, the salesman knows he really hasn't lost a thing. The salesman can now spend his time elsewhere, talking to more reasonable and *more profitable* prospects.

State your one-time price to the "price buyers." Mean it! Be polite but firm. Your prospect will know that you are serious about your price and will either accept or reject your proposition. The world is full of prospects who are willing to pay a fair and reasonable price for your product. Why should you waste your time on a man who is trying to chisel and take all the profit out of your sale?

The next time you're tempted to cut your price, remember the story about the salesman who lost a nickel on every sale but who supposedly made up for it in increased volume. Don't believe it! *It can't be done!*

When you're forced to "horse trade"

In some industries, dickering over the price has become an accepted practice. This practice began, I think, when the first three-toed horse was traded by a caveman. And we still see its modernized version in the automobile showroom where prospective customers invariably make counteroffers to the salesman's price quotations.

Haggling over price has spread to many other industries and it's not uncommon to see buyers and sellers of every type of product, from scrap metal to food commodities, engaged in friendly debate over the price to be paid.

What should a salesman do when he's forced to make a "price adjustment?" Let's look at the price adjustment technique used by many auto salesmen who exemplify modern horse-trading at its best.

What happens when there is a $200 difference in the price thinking of a car salesman and his prospect? Does the salesman offer to split the difference? Usually not. The salesman knows that if he does cut his price in half, the prospect will expect the price to be cut in half again.

When the professional car salesman backs away from his price he'll do it by quoting odd dollars. He may, for example, ask for $183 difference instead of the original $200 difference, a reduction of $17. What's the prospect's normal reaction to this *small, odd* reduction in price? "This salesman," the prospect is thinking, "is probably close to his rock-bottom price or he would have cut his price more than this small amount."

Note that the old pro salesman avoided the use of even numbers. There were no 10s, 20s or 50s in his revised offer. He left the impression that he had used a very sharp pencil to squeeze out that $17 and take it off the original price. Odd figures are usually accepted by a prospect as a sign that you've done all you can to lower the price and that he'd better accept your offer before you change your mind.

When you're forced to adjust price, remember this simple technique of using odd figures and reducing your price in small amounts. The whole objective of selling is not to move merchandise, *it's to make a profit.*

Words can close sales

Listen to the words professional salesmen use when they're closing a sale. One word will be used more often than any other. This is so because that one word is the most powerful word in any closing situation. That almost magical word is "why."

"*Why* do you say that, Mr. Prospect?"

"*Why* do you hesitate, Mr. Prospect?"

"*Why* isn't today the best time to buy this product, Mr. Prospect?"

"Why" is the one word that requires the prospect to become a part of the closing effort. That one powerful "why" just can't be ignored. It demands an answer. It brings unknown objections out into the open where they can be discussed, discounted, and dismissed.

Ask your prospect "why?" and he'll have to start talking. Now he's an active participant in the close. Now he'll have to reveal his thoughts and intentions. Now his own attention is focused on the subject the salesman wants to talk about — the closing of the sale.

Try this experiment

If you doubt the power of this single word, "why," try this interesting experiment. Ask your wife or luncheon companion a question. When they answer, ask, "Why did you answer that way?" Keep asking "why?" time after time and watch the reaction. Your wife or luncheon companion will be doing all the talking. Your part in the conversation will consist mostly of the single word "why."

"Why" is an action word. Use it in the closing room and you can get to the root of any problem that's standing in the way of a sale.

Another word you'll hear frequently in the closing room is "amazing."

"This is an *amazing* product, Mr. Prospect."

"It's *amazing* how this product fits your exact needs, Mr. Prospect."

"Amazing" is a word that generates excitement. "Startling" is another. Put these two words together in a sentence, say the sentence out loud, and try to avoid excitement in your voice:

"Here are some *startling* facts about this *amazing* product, Mr. Prospect."

You can sense the excitement you've put into this single sentence. Your prospects won't yawn when you confront them with statements such as this. These are excitement builders, and that's exactly the emotion you're trying to evoke. You're trying to get your prospect excited about buying your product.

Words create enthusiasm

A favorite combination of words used by successful closers are the words "at last."

"After years of testing we've found the answer *at last*."

"*At last* we've designed a welder that will join every type of metal you use in your shop."

It is difficult to say these sentences out loud without sensing a feeling of excitement within yourself. Excitement is contagious. Excitement builds enthusiasm. And contagious enthusiasm will move prospects to take positive action.

Professional closers have other favorite closing words that add sparkle and power to their requests for the order. Here are 12 words which you can use to close more sales and make more money:

Money	Result	Love
You	Health	Discover
Save	Safety	Proven
New	Easy	Guarantee

"Own this product and you'll *discover* a *new love* of life, *health,* and happiness such as you've never experienced before." Is this a dull and unprovocative sentence? Not at all! It's packed with words that can make you a more effective closer.

Use these words when you're trying to close sales and I'll *guarantee* that you'll be a more successful closer than you ever dreamed possible.

Seven ways to close that sale

Interviews with successful closers reveal that there are surprising similarities in the methods and techniques they employ. Boiled down to their essentials, there are exactly seven basic techniques used by the professionals to lock up an order:

1. *Assume the prospect wants to buy today.* Successful closers always assume that the prospect not only wants their product but that he also is ready to buy — today! The salesman knows that if the prospect has listened to the complete sales presentation, offered no unanswered objections, and has both an interest and a preference for the product, he is ready to be closed. He wants to buy now. So, the only thing to be done is to sit down with the prospect, go over the details, and get his "OK" on the order form.

This is what is known as the assumptive key to the close. This is the positive attitude that disarms the prospect. This is the attitude which makes it easier for the prospect to say yes than to say no. It's an attitude that closes sales.

2. *Ask the prospect to agree with you.* When you're trying to close a sale, the first yes is often the most difficult to wring from a prospect. So, the professional salesman begins by asking the prospect to agree with simple, noncommittal questions, such as: "This is a nice-looking set of hand tools, isn't it, Mr. Prospect?"

The prospect knows he can agree with the salesman on this question without committing himself. The salesman has made it easy for him to agree — and difficult for him to disagree. The normal prospect reaction is a "yes" answer.

Next, the salesman seeks additional agreement to progressively more important questions:

"These hand tools would make your job easier, wouldn't they, Mr. Prospect?"

"Wouldn't it be a pleasure to open your tool box tomorrow morning and find this new set of tools ready and waiting to go to work for you?"

It's always easier to say yes when you're in the habit of saying yes. Thus, the professional closer always works up to that final "yes, I'll buy" with the technique of obtaining little agreements en route.

3. *Refer to impending events.* When a prospect says he isn't ready to buy today, the professional closer will often begin to talk about an impending event. Something important is about to happen and that something makes today the best time to buy.

The price may be changed by the factory (the salesman heard a rumor to this effect only yesterday). You can make this guarantee only if the prospect buys the product today. Another buyer is interested in purchasing this last machine in your local warehouse.

If the prospect is really ready to be closed, the mere mention of an impending event is a powerful motivator to induce him to take action today.

4. *Take some physical action.* You've tried to close the sale and failed. Silence reigns. You've hit a temporary impasse. What can be done to get his signature on the order?

One very successful closing technique is to quietly put the order form and pen in front of the prospect *and then do nothing.* This is a pressure tactic — a real pressure tactic. You're standing there with folded arms. You're not talking. You're looking him straight in the eye. The pressure is on. He has to do something to relieve this pressure. The simplest and easiest out for the prospect is to sign the order. And he frequently does.

Many salesmen, however, prefer not to use such a high pressure tactic when closing a sale. But they do understand that when an impasse is reached, something must be done. So, they try some other form of physical action. They'll shuffle their demonstration papers, reach into a briefcase for another brochure, or even rise from their chairs to get a drink of water. Physical action will break the strain of a nothing-is-happening situation and can often turn the prospect's indecision into decision.

5. *Offer an inducement.* You believe the prospect is almost ready to buy. You want to close the sale today. But your prospect may have a "want" of his own. He may want to feel that he is getting special, preferential treatment.

So, okay, — give it to him. Offer him some special inducement to sign the order today. Try a month's free maintenance service for the machine *if* he'll sign today. Offer him a lengthened warranty period, an optional equipment item added at no extra cost *if he'll buy today.*

The inducement you offer should be something small and inexpensive. You're not buying his business. You're only returning his favor — the one he's doing for you by signing the order today. Make him feel that he's getting a real bargain by taking action today. You'll be surprised at how many extra sales you can close by providing preferential treatment (the kind that doesn't give away your profit).

6. *Talk about other happy buyers.* Your prospect knows that if other people use your product and are satisfied with it, he will probably like it, too. If the other people are celebrities or leaders in the local business community, your prospect will want to identify with them. Therefore, help him identify.

Tell your prospect about the other man who had the same need for the product, bought it, and is now glad that he did. This if-others-like-it-I-should-too syndrome has been used to close many a sale when all other methods have failed.

7. *Ask for that order.* Have a written proposal or completed order form in hand whenever you try to close.

Assume that the prospect intends to sign today. If you ask him to sign, the chances are favorable that he will.

The prospect is well aware that you're a salesman. He knows you make you living from completed sales. He understands that your presentations, demonstrations, and all of your sales calls have been made with one objective in mind: you want him to buy your product. Thus, it will come as no surprise to him if you ask for the order. He'll only be surprised if you don't.

Can you remember the last time a salesman appeared hesitant to ask you for an order? Was your reaction a positive or negative one? Chances are your thoughts ran something like this: "Why should I spend my money for this salesman's product if he hasn't got the nerve to ask me to buy it? Is he ashamed of his product?" Questions such as these just naturally pop up in a prospect's mind when he's ready to buy and the salesman doesn't ask for the order.

Remember — you've worked hard to prepare for this moment. The prospect is ready, *so ask him to buy.*

The simple secret of closing sales

What makes a man say yes or no when you ask him to buy your product or service? It isn't the question you ask or the closing technique you use. If a man isn't interested in your product and has no desire for it, the most effective closing technique in the world isn't going to work for you.

The secret to closing lies in the fact that your prospect's yes or no is determined by all the things you've said and done *before* you ask for the order. If you have successfully contacted a man with the need for your product and the ability to buy it, sparked his interest in it, created preference for it, *and have the courage to ask for his order,* he has no alternative but to say yes.

Closing is not a strange and mysterious art in itself. Closing is merely the last step in a well-organized and well-presented sales story told to a man with need, purchasing ability, and desire which you, with a programmed sales effort, have implanted in his mind.

This, then, is the apparent magic in The Golden Stairway to Successful Sales. Each step in the sales effort, successfully completed, supports the next, and the end result, like a well-constructed building, is cemented together with the closing of the sale. The final building block in a successfully constructed sale fits easily into place when you *ask for the order*.

The big man at the last is the man who takes an idea and makes it a genuine success — the man who brings the ship into port.

— Elbert Hubbard

Psycho-Sales-Analysis Guide

*After reading Section 9, write
your answers to these questions:*

1. What are some questions I can ask to evoke a "yes" answer from my prospects?

2. When is the best time to quote the price of my product or service?

3. What price-quoting statement can I use to minimize the chance of creating a price objection?

4. What are six positive, excitement-provoking words I can use when asking for the order? Use these words in a sample closing statement and underline the excitement-provoking words.

5. What can I say that will offer my prospects:

    a. An inducement to buy today?

    b. A testimonial to induce them to buy today?

    c. An impending event to make them buy today?

6. Remembering a recent unsuccessful close attempt:

    a. Why didn't this man buy?

    b. What could I have said or done to have saved this sale?

7. What is my strongest closing technique?

8. What is my weakest closing technique?

9. What steps can I take to strengthen my weakest closing technique?

10. In order of their importance, what are three things I can do to become a more successful closer?

Section 10

Psycho-Sales-Analysis Guide

Before reading Section 10, write your answers to these questions:

1. What percent of my customers are fully satisfied with and enthusiastic about my products or service?

2. What are the three most frequently-expressed after-sale complaints of my customers?

3. Recalling a recent lost customer, why was he lost?

4. What might I have done to have prevented the loss of this customer?

5. What is the average time lapse between contacts with my customers?

6. How do I rate myself *(poor, fair,* or *excellent)* in the following areas?

    a. Interest in customer welfare.

    b. Rapport with customers.

    c. Preventing customer dissatisfaction.

    d. Handling complaints.

    e. Helping customers get maximum benefit from the products I sell.

Building repeat sales

An old cliché in the selling profession states that "a good salesman never really starts to sell until the prospect says no." Today, in our highly competitive economy, this statement should be expanded by adding: "and he never stops selling."

Today's selling professional acknowledges the completion of a sale as a stepping-stone to greater achievements — the chance to sell again and again — and to keep selling to more and more people. The professional selling man knows that until the customer is happily using the product the sale is incomplete. So the old pro in selling does everything he can to make certain the product he sells is being properly used and that a happy customer is using it.

How can you be sure that your customers are getting maximum utilization from your product, and that they'll buy again — from *you*? The answer, of course, lies in maintaining contact with your customers and providing the type of follow-up service you would like to have if you were the customer.

There are, as an example, a number of techniques which professional salesmen use to take care of their customers. It's only the "pitch men" who sell them and leave them. The professional knows that it's far better (and far more profitable) to sell them and service them.

While it's not always possible to be present at the time your product is delivered to a customer, it is advisable to be. And there are a number of very good reasons why personal delivery of the product (especially high ticket items) can help a salesman build repeat sales:

- *You* have the customer's confidence.
- *You* are the one who made the sale.
- *You* are the one who will collect the commission.
- *You* represent the company in your customer's eyes.

  And most important of all,

- *You* stand to benefit the most from a happy customer.

Regardless of the product you sell, it will pay you to make a special event of the delivery. If your product was shipped or mailed, you can telephone, telegraph, or write your customer. Time your message so that he will hear from you on the day he receives the product. You'll be letting him know that you are still interested in his welfare even though you already have his order and his money. You can let him know that you still have an interest in his gaining all the benefits you promised him. You'd be flattered by such extra service and attention, wouldn't you? So will your customer!

If it's possible to be present when your product is delivered, make sure your customer knows all he needs to know about it and how it operates. If it's a mechanical item, turn it on, let it run, and be sure everything is working properly.

Is your product one that's built to the customer's specifications? While the prospect is waiting for his order, follow the lead of a well-known shipbuilder who takes periodic photos of his customer's ship as it's being constructed. "Here's how your new ship looks this week," says the letter accompanying the photograph. What's the customer's natural reaction to this special attention? "The salesman who sold me this ship is still interested in *me*!" When this customer is ready for his next ship, and the next, which salesman do you think will get the order? (Do your regular customers feel this strongly about you?)

Handle complaints promptly and fairly

If your customer voices a complaint, don't ignore it. That complaint isn't going to evaporate into thin air. It can only grow in size and get worse.

Can you remember how unhappy you were when the cigarette lighter didn't work in that new car you bought? Every time you tried to use the lighter you became angry. And you probably began to notice many other small things about your new car that also weren't right. One small complaint can build itself into major dissatisfaction.

Even when the customer's complaint appears small to you, remember that it can be a very important thing in his mind. Listen to this complaint. If the gripe is justified, take up the battle in the customer's behalf. If he isn't justified in his complaint, be frank and honest with him. You have to be fair to your company, too. When in doubt, put yourself in the customer's shoes, then try on the company's shoes, and handle the complaint as promptly and fairly as you can.

Stay in touch with your customers

Is your product one which is used up or eventually wears out and must be replaced? Keeping in contact with your customers is an excellent way to insure future sales.

Do you have a personal calendar follow-up system? Most successful salesmen do. Here, for example, is the follow-up schedule used by a very successful road grader salesman:

One week after the order is signed he writes a "thank you" letter to his customer.

One week before delivery of the product he writes his customer to say that he'll be present at the delivery — and he always is!

Three days after the delivery he telephones his customer to be sure the machine is working properly.

One week after the delivery he sends another "thank you" letter which invites the customer to telephone collect if any maintenance, service, or warranty problems should occur.

Three months after the delivery he invites his customer to lunch. While eating lunch he also asks if any other road grader users have expressed an interest in the customer's new machine. He's fishing for new prospects as well as taking care of an old customer.

Six months after the delivery he makes a personal call at the customer's office "to see how you and your road grader are getting along." Once again he asks about any other prospective customers who have seen the machine.

One year after the delivery he mails a birthday card "to road grader K677946Z" in care of its owner. This humorous approach reminds the customer that his machine is now one year old and that it may be time for a replacement. A follow-up sales call is then made to initiate the sale of a replacement machine.

Follow-up programs increase sales

Will such a follow-up program result in increased sales? This salesman is convinced that it does. He's sold more than $1 million worth of road construction equipment each year for the past 12 years. This salesman is now so busy on his follow-up programs to present customers (and selling them replacement equipment) that he complains about not having time to find and work new prospects. This professional salesman knows that people prefer to buy from friends rather than strangers. He takes care of his customers and they, in turn, take care of him. It's a very profitable arrangement.

Road graders are not the only products to be successfully sold with a programmed follow-up. Repeat sales of chemicals, lathes, and washroom soap dispensers are being made today because their salesmen designed and used effective follow-up programs. "Even though I have your order, I'm still vitally interested in you and your problems," the salesman's actions say. And actions still speak louder than words.

Stay in touch with prospects

While we're on the subject of present customers, let's not forget those future customers — your prospects. Staying in touch with potential buyers is just as important as staying in touch with customers.

An airplane dealer friend of mine had an insurance salesman for a customer. This customer was an aviation booster and was so interested in flying that he made arrangements for no less than 15 of his friends to fly in the dealer's demonstrator airplane.

The dealer discounted this interest and wrote off his time and expense as a favor to his insurance salesman customer. He ignored those 15 riders. Some months afterward he was chagrined to discover that 7 of the 15 had purchased competitive brand airplanes after flying in his demonstrator. His failure to follow up and to stay in touch with these riders had cost him dearly.

Is there an easy and inexpensive way to remain in touch with both customers and prospects? Yes, there certainly is. It's a weapon that's won many a sales battle. It's called a postcard.

The next time you're out on the road, buy a batch of picture postcards. Then, instead of propping your feet up on the bed and watching television in the motel at night, write notes on these postcards to your prospects and customers. Send one to the prospect you called on in the last town.

"Certainly enjoyed our brief visit. Thought of you tonight when I saw this scene."

It's not so much the message that counts, it's the thought. Now your prospect (or customer) will remember you as the salesman who actually took the time to sit down and write a postcard. Who else sends him postcards? His *friends* do. And what have you done with this simple act of writing a postcard? You've put yourself in his circle of friends. You'll be remembered when you call at his office again. And you'll be remembered not as a salesman but as a friend! Try it. It's a technique that's both surprising and rewarding.

Help your customers make better use of your product

Are your present customers getting the most benefits they can from the products you've sold to them? Do the users or operators know the fine points of your product? How about the purchasing agent who bought it? Should more employees in a particular company be using your product? If you can show additional need through increased usage you'll stand a good chance of getting additional orders.

Some salesmen make the serious mistake of thinking that once they've gotten the order, the product is sold. Customer service is now someone else's worry. Believe me, it isn't!

Keep a follow-up notebook

Henry C. Garvey is a very successful salesman. His products are printing presses which sell upwards of $250,000 per unit. Henry knows and uses selling basics. But his success, I've decided, is primarily due to the extra care and attention Henry gives to his customers.

Some years ago, Henry showed me his follow-up notebook. "I'm always on the lookout for new ways to help my customers," Henry told me. "When I find a new idea that will help me do a better job of follow-up, I write it down in this notebook. Once a month I try to use at least one of these ideas on each of my customers. It helps me stay in touch with them and they know I haven't forgotten them."

You'll find adaptations of Henry's idea used by professionals in almost every field of selling. You can use this idea to build and expand your own sales. All you have to do is keep your eyes and ears open, remain alert to competitive activities, write down your follow-up ideas as they come to you, and then use them.

Here are several follow-up techniques to help you start your own personal follow-up notebook:

Use personal notes instead of formal business letters when writing to your customers and prospects. This technique is one which will help transform cold business relationships into warm friendships. Customers and prospects prefer to buy from their friends.

Send new product literature as soon as it's off the press. Your customers will want to be kept up-to-date on all product developments.

Mail trade clippings and photocopies of these clippings to your customers. Magazine articles about their business, and news of competitors, new products, or developments in their business area are always welcome. Your local letter service can provide inexpensive copies if they're needed.

Send free samples and trade-show "give-aways" by mail with your calling card. Put these items in your customers' hands before they attend the trade shows.

Supply sales leads to your customers. Even if they're already aware of the prospect, they'll appreciate the interest you have taken in their business.

Send birthday cards to your important customers. This is what a friend would do. The date? Your customer's secretary will be glad to supply this information if you ask for it. And there's always a copy of *Who's Who* in the library.

Praise your customers and prospects when praise is due. Did his company's stock experience a substantial gain, his annual report show increased earnings, or did his firm receive a large government order? Watch the financial progress and other successes enjoyed by your customers. Let them know that you are vitally interested in their progress.

The customer who rightfully or wrongfully feels that the salesman's only interest is in getting the order is not likely to buy again from him. Customers are people, too! They appreciate attention. Give it to them. Repeat business, new business leads, and many other benefits will come to you if you take the time to follow the old Golden Rule and treat customers as you yourself would like to be treated.

As a wise man once said: Business goes where it is invited and stays where it is well treated.

The longer I live, the more deeply I am convinced that that which makes the difference between one man and another — between the weak and the powerful, the great and the insignificant — is energy, invincible determination, and a purpose well formed.

— Elbert Hubbard

Psycho-Sales-Analysis Guide

*After reading Section 10, write
your answers to these questions:*

1. How can I assist in the delivery of my product or make deliveries more of a special event?

2. What can I do to insure that prospect complaints are handled more promptly and more fairly?

3. What time schedule should I follow and what should I do to provide improved follow-up service for my customers?

4. How can I help my customers gain more benefit from the products they purchase from me?

5. What after-sale service ideas can I borrow from:

    a. My competition?

    b. Other industries?

Section 11

Psycho-Sales-Analysis Guide

*Before reading Section 11, write
your answers to these questions:*

1. Who helps me with the preparation of my proposals?

2. What items do I normally include in written proposals?

3. If asked for a description of my sales manager, what would I say?

4. Is it really important for me to have good rapport with plant and office associates? Explain in detail.

5. How do I rate *(poor, fair,* or *excellent)* in these areas?

    a. Friendly attitude.

    b. Loyalty to my company.

    c. Response to instructions.

    d. Response to suggestions.

    e. Open-mindedness.

    f. In-plant communications.

    g. Report writing.

    h. Ability to get along with:

        1) Sales manager.   4) Secretaries.

        2) Engineers.   5) Other salesmen.

        3) Production people.

Working with the sales team

SALESMEN are a rugged breed. They prefer to work alone. They enjoy the challenge of solitary, face-to-face "combat" with prospective buyers. Put them behind an office desk, at the engineer's drawing board, or on the factory production line and they'll be unhappy and frustrated. They are men of action — singlehanded action.

In many ways the modern salesman is much like the "lonesome end" on a football team. He's excluded from the office "huddle." He's physically separated from his teammates, and he often has to play out his role without his teammates' physical support. Despite this fact, the salesman's success or failure is, nonetheless, dependent on *team effort.*

The mature salesman is one who recognizes the importance of the other members of the sales team. He knows that engineers must plan properly before a salable product can be produced. The production people must follow the engineered design and produce on schedule, or late deliveries and lost orders will result. The advertising and sales promotion experts must presell before volume sales can be achieved. Without the full support of the home office and factory, a salesman simply cannot achieve his maximum success in a competitive market. This is why today's successful salesman is more of a team player than an individual star.

It's most unfortunate that many capable salesmen are less successful than they could be simply because they do not feel it sufficiently important to take the time to sell themselves within their own organizations. It's important for the salesman to win and hold the backing of production managers, shipping personnel, engineers, sales managers, and sales secretaries. Knowing when and how to ask for such help is a mark of the mature, selling professional.

Ask others to help with your proposals

There's always a sense of personal achievement in being known as a do-it-yourself salesman. But pride has been the undoing of many a salesman who presented an incomplete, incorrect, or less-than-the-best proposal in a competitive situation. There's no consolation prize or award of merit when the best man and the best product are represented by a second-best proposal.

If you've ever had to return to a customer's office and ask him to re-sign an order because your original figures were incorrect, you'll understand the real meaning of embarrassment. What's worse, your customer may have second thoughts about signing again. One such experience will convince the most independent salesman that he should *always* have his written presentation figures checked by the office staff *before* they're presented to the prospect.

Product performance and other technical matters should be reviewed by engineers before they're included in proposals. If legal problems are involved, the firm's lawyers should be called in for consultation. Delivery dates should be confirmed with production managers before commitments are made. A competitive proposal must be a team effort.

The salesman's best friend could well be the engineer who corrects a mistaken specification, the production manager who wisely advances the delivery date, the accountant who discovers an omitted sales tax, or the secretary who retypes the proposal cover because the prospect's name was misspelled. The professional salesman uses the talents of the professionals in other fields to augment his own skills.

Most companies have developed standard formats for their proposals. However, alert salesmen can often borrow successful ideas used by the competition and other industries to make their written proposals more effective. Here, for example, are a number of suggestions obtained from seminars attended by many of the nation's most successful marketing experts:

- Use quality paper stock.

- Invest in an attractive cover.

- Imprint the cover with the name of the recipient and his company.

- Include an inside cover page containing the name of the salesman, his company, and his telephone number. The prospect may have questions or want to mail in the order. Make certain he knows where and to whom to send the order.

- Consider the inclusion of the following:

1) Product brochure pages.
2) Photographs.
3) Detailed price and warranty information.
4) A review of the benefits your product offers to the prospect. Be sure to include benefits the prospect feels are important.
5) A brief history of the demonstrations you've made and the prospect's favorable reactions at that time.
6) Charts, graphs, maps, and other visuals to tell your story in picture fashion.
7) A specific request for the signed order.

It should be mentioned that different people buy your product for different reasons. Thus, a stock proposal, one that is the same for each prospect, cannot be as effective as an individually tailored proposal, one that spells out the benefits that this prospect is interested in and wants. The extra time you spend in preparing a better proposal can be time well spent.

Working with the sales manager

Most of the problems which arise between salesmen and sales managers, I've discovered, can be quickly and easily solved when *attitudes* are corrected. There's an almost natural tendency on the part of every salesman to fear or resent the sales manager's authority. But the simple fact remains that both the salesman's future and the sales manager's future are inexorably tied together. One cannot succeed without the other. Therefore, the professional salesman takes time to sell himself to his sales manager and keep the communication channels open.

If you'd like to establish and maintain better working relations with your sales management, here are six things you can do. If you'll follow these suggestions I can personally guarantee that you'll not only enjoy your job more but that you'll be more successful in your selling career.

1. *Remember that sales managers are human beings.* Sales managers are neither gods nor ogres. They are human beings with human ambitions, human emotions, human needs, and human wants. They are not infallible and they *are* capable of making a mistake now and then.

Thus, if you're occasionally treated in a manner that you consider to be unfair, don't over-react. Your sales manager can have an off day, too. He's entitled to be grumpy once in a while. Remember this and wait for a more opportune time before presenting your side of a disagreement.

2. *Find out what the sales manager wants, then help him get it!* Your sales manager has his own goals and ambitions. He wants to be recognized as the team leader. He is probably seeking advancement within the company. If you can help him reach his personal goals, you'll be his friend for life. And when he does vacate the sales manager's chair, it just might fit you!

3. *Don't procrastinate on paper work.* Perhaps the most common area of disagreement between salesmen and sales managers involves paperwork. Salesmen hate paperwork. They'll go to almost any extreme to avoid it.

Always remember that the sales manager needs your reports if he is to do his job properly. If he doesn't know what you are doing he can't very well help you do a better job. So, follow the rules and play the game fairly. Get your paperwork done right and in on time.

4. *Correct misunderstandings promptly.* Misunderstandings and disagreements won't vanish just because they are ignored. They'll only grow and intensify. So face up to misunderstandings. Talk to your sales manager politely and respectfully. Explain your thoughts and opinions. But be prepared to accept the sales manager's decision as final. He's the leader of the sales force and there's only one quarterback allowed on the team.

5. *Treat the sales manager as a VIP.* Your sales manager is a very important person (VIP) in your life. Your sales career is largely dependent on his opinion of your sales performance. So accord him the respect his position deserves.

Before you were hired you went to great lengths to impress your sales manager and you sold yourself by using your very best sales techniques. Is there any reason why you shouldn't keep selling yourself? There isn't. Without a well-satisfied sales manager, there's very little opportunity for you to gain personal advancement in your present company.

6. *Be kind to the sales manager's secretary.* There's usually a close business relationship established between the sales manager and his secretary. They share the same confidences, work closely together, and are likely to develop a protective bond between them. So never speak disrespectfully of one in front of the other, and show proper deference to the secretary. Ladies are also subject to that business malady called "rank happiness."

With the joint approval of the sales manager and his secretary, you may be able to get valuable secretarial aid for the asking. Perhaps the secretary can update some of your records while you're out making calls. Perhaps she can make appointments in your behalf, write sales letters, and do many of those other detailed chores that take valuable time away from your selling day. Let her do your office work while you concentrate on getting those orders.

Look around at the successful salesmen. You'll find they usually have an excellent rapport established with their sales manager's secretary. They know she is in a key position to help or hinder their progress. They treat her as a VIP because she is one!

A word about those hard-to-understand engineers

Quite often it's the engineer who causes the biggest headaches in a salesman's life and many salesmen are prone to view their own company's engineering staff as the enemy camp and a haven for uncommunicative introverts. Engineers, in turn, are likely to see salesmen as overly-talkative, overly-gregarious and under-productive. It would appear that there is a natural communications barrier between these two professions despite the fact that their futures are intertwined and one cannot attain job security without the services of the other.

The success-oriented salesman understands that he needs the help of his company's engineers. Their advice and counsel is important for his proposals. They can change (or refuse to change) design features that will make a product easier to sell. Frequently, the engineering mind, viewing marketing problems from a detached point of view, can assist the salesman by pointing out such things as competitive product limitations the salesman has not seen.

There are a number of things a salesman can do to establish and maintain an improved rapport with the engineering department. Suggestions from the field for product improvement will be welcomed by the engineers *if* they are properly presented. ("Why weren't you guys smart enough to think of this yourselves?" is not the proper way.)

Inviting engineers to attend sales meetings is an excellent way to help them understand marketing problems. Asking for advice (even if the advice isn't followed) will help engineers feel they are recognized as members of the selling team. In short, the successful salesman is one who recognizes the importance of his company's engineers and takes the time to sell them and keep them sold as a part of his in-depth selling program.

Production managers respond to kindness, too

No product is ever sold until it is in the hands of a satisfied user. The salesman who has lost a sale because the product couldn't be delivered will understand the awful truth of this statement. He'll also understand the importance of maintaining close liaison with the production department.

Sometimes, in their eagerness to obtain an order, inexperienced salesmen will promise unrealistic or even impossible delivery dates. The result is almost always an angry production manager, an unhappy customer, and an unhappy salesman with lost business. Therefore, take time to check with the production department whenever there's a question about delivery schedules. It's a common courtesy to both your customer and the production people who are an important part of your team.

Remember, please, that production managers have their problems, too. Personnel turnover on the production line, late deliveries of vendor-supplied items, training and retraining when design changes occur — their problems are almost endless. So when you find less-than-perfect quality control, or even a gross error committed by the production or shipping departments, treat your factory teammates with the same courtesy you extend to prospects and customers. You're the selling expert, remember? A little salesmanship at the home office and plant can make your outside selling easier, more enjoyable, and more profitable to you.

Don't forget advertising and promotion people

Your advertising and sales promotion people are also VIP members of the team. Because they're creative people they're apt to be more sensitive than average. Help them by supplying copies of competitive literature and bringing back suggestions from the field. But be careful about telling them how to do their jobs. They're the experts in their field just as you are in yours. It's true that they probably haven't had your experiences in the field — but give them full credit for knowing their business and being professionals.

There's one point, I believe, which needs to be stressed. In dealing with your associates at the factory and office, you needn't roll over and play dead when their opinions are different than yours. You're not engaged in a popularity contest. You have a job that needs to be done. There will be times when you'll have to be firm to do that job. You'll have to stand up for what's right instead of for what will make the boss, the production managers, or the engineers happy. You can do this, hold your own self-respect, and gain their respect in the bargain by selling your thoughts and opinions in a professional manner.

Lastly, and certainly not least, you should occasionally take a self-inventory and appraise your personal sales performance as it's seen by your company's general management. Have you been too prone to cut prices and give away profits? Have your expense accounts been creeping upward? Have you been taking longer and longer lunch hours and extra days off from work? It's true that how well you are doing your job isn't nearly as important to your future with your present company as *how other people, particularly management people, believe you are doing your job.* It's management's impressions, not the facts, which determine your advancement or lack of advancement in your company.

I'm sure you've recognized that what we've been discussing is nothing more than basic psychology and the art of getting along with people. As a professional salesman you know how to do this. What you need to keep in mind is that the home office and factory members of your sales team are people, too. They'll respond to the same selling techniques that you use on your prospects and customers. And you can move yourself forward toward greater success by taking the time to sell yourself to your teammates.

A challenge you may not dare to accept

You're a salesman, a professional salesman. You know how to convince people that they should buy the products you sell. Right?

Let's see just how good a salesman you are.

Let's see if you can sell yourself to the one individual in your own company who presently thinks least of your sales abilities — that's the guy who doesn't like you.

I'd suggest you start with sales step number one, prospecting. Do your research and find out what it is this man is seeking in life. Then proceed through the sales steps. Contact him. Arouse his interest in you (while "unarousing" his dislikes). Help him develop a preference for your friendship. Ask for his friendship — and then "close the sale" by making him your friend.

It won't be easy. You're starting with a built-in handicap — his present distaste for you and/or your ability as a salesman.

But anyone can be sold if he's approached by a real selling professional, right?

Before cooperation comes in any line, there is always competition pushed to a point that threatens destruction and promises chaos; then to avert ruin, man devises a better way, a plan that conserves and economizes, and behold it is found in cooperation.

— *Elbert Hubbard*

Psycho-Sales-Analysis Guide

*After reading Section 11, write
your answers to these questions:*

1. What member of the sales team has the least respect for me as a salesman and a person?

2. What is the real cause for the poor rapport in question 1?

3. What steps can I take to correct this situation?

4. Everyone makes mistakes when dealing with other people. What is the biggest error I have made in dealing with the people on my sales team?

5. What is the single most-important step I can take to make other sales team members want to help me succeed in my job as a salesman?

Section 12

Psycho-Sales-Analysis Guide

*Before reading Section 12, write
your answers to these questions:*

1. What percent of my time am I now spending:

   a. Planning and making reports?

   b. Getting ready to sell?

   c. Traveling and waiting to see prospects and customers?

   d. Conducting face-to-face selling?

2. What daily activities take time away from my selling activities? (No one is perfect. We all waste some time and now's the time to be honest with yourself — it's all for your benefit.) Make a list of the time-wasting activities and the amount of time lost per day.

3. How do I rate *(poor, fair,* or *excellent)* in these areas?

   a. Reporting to work on time.

   b. Putting in a full day.

   c. Making the maximum number of calls each day.

   d. Working extra hours if required.

4. Does the most successful salesman I know:

   a. Work longer hours than I do?

   b. Make more sales calls than I do?

   c. Plan his sales day more efficiently than I do?

How to make
better use of your time

ALL MEN are created equal. This statement from the Declaration of Independence has fired the hearts of mankind, and ranks, along with the Golden Rule, among the most loved and compassionate utterances of all time. *But is it really true?*

If we're practical in our thinking we'll have to admit that heredity and environment shape our individual lives, and that each of us, as individuals, has vastly different potential and capabilities. Physical imperfections, different social backgrounds, varying educational opportunities and achievements — these and countless other differences make us very *un*equal.

Yet there's one factor of equality that all men share and share alike: each man has the same 24 hours in each day at his disposal. Time is the one and only common denominator. No man has more hours in his day and no man has less. It's how each man uses his 24 hours that determines the degree of success he will attain in his lifetime.

Since we're talking about salesmanship, let's consider success or failure in terms of selling. To be a successful salesman one must sell, and the degree of success a salesman attains will depend on the amount of goods or services sold.

How does a salesman increase his chances of making a sale? He does this by putting himself in front of another individual who has the need and ability to buy the product the salesman is selling. It is, therefore, obvious that the more time you spend talking to prospects (the legitimate type) the greater will be your chance for success.

A look at a working day

Is there room for improvement in *your* selling-time habits? Let's look at the way the average American salesman spends his working hours as reported by a recent nationwide survey.

A salesman isn't making money while he's traveling between interviews, preparing plans or reports, or getting ready to sell. The money-making time in a salesman's day is the time he spends in face-to-face contact with a prospect.

How can this face-to-face selling time be increased? The salesman might refine his prospecting and planning methods and thereby shorten his getting-ready-to-sell time. But this 23% of his time is probably necessary if he is to qualify his prospects properly and do all the other important things that getting ready implies.

What about planning and reports? Can the salesman save time here and apply that time to face-to-face selling activities? Again, this 18% of his time represents a vital and necessary part of a well-organized sales program. There's really not much chance to save time in this area.

If the average American salesman wants to rearrange his time expenditures to find more time for face-to-face selling, there are only two things he can do: He can work longer hours, or he can shorten the time he is now spending *between* interviews.

The first alternative (working longer hours) is not a popular one except with a few sales managers I've known and worked for. The professional salesman needs his rest and recreation. He likes to play golf or fish just as other men

THE AVERAGE AMERICAN SALESMAN'S SELLING DAY

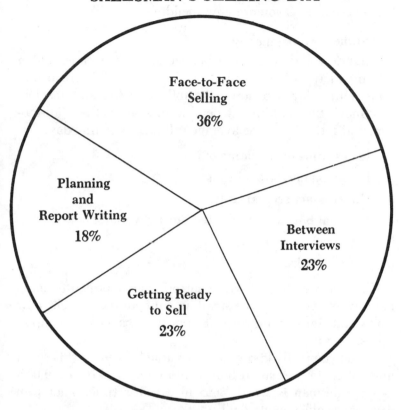

Face-to-Face
Selling
36%

Planning
and
Report Writing
18%

Between
Interviews
23%

Getting Ready
to Sell
23%

do. So, instead of deciding to work longer hours, he looks to the between-interview time as the best and most logical area for time saving. If he can reorganize himself and his selling program, perhaps he can spend more time talking with prospects and still have some time left to spend with his family and friends in recreational activities.

Let's take another look at the chart. You'll note that almost one-fourth of the average salesman's day is spent between calls. It's true that time must be spent in traveling from one prospect's office to another and waiting in the outer offices. But you do *not* have to spend as much time in these activities as you are now spending.

Your time is worth money

What do you do with your between-interview time? Other salesmen have a habit of letting "time-wasters" creep into their selling day. Go down the following list and see just how much time *you* might be able to save in these all-too-common activities in the average salesman's selling day.

1. Excess time in the home office.
2. Poorly planned travel routes.
3. Unnecessary second calls.
4. Personal business conducted during working hours.
5. Extended lunch hours.
6. Coffee breaks.

If you've been honest with yourself, you've probably noted areas where you can save small amounts of time. Right now this small time-saving doesn't appear to have much importance, does it?

But do you really know the true value (to you) of this small amount of time? A small half-hour a day saved by a $10,000-a-year salesman is worth $625 in a year's time. That's an expensive coffee break, isn't it?

Look at the Time Value Chart on page 181 and you'll discover that even a few minutes a day are worth many dollars in a year's time. Remember that this chart considers only the value of working hours. It doesn't talk about the value of selling hours. Selling hours are those money-making hours you spend face-to-face with a prospect.

The value of working hours and selling hours is considerably different. If, for example, a salesman works a 40-

hour week to make $15,000, the value of each of his *working* hours would be $7.50. If this same salesman spends only 25% of his working time in face-to-face selling activities, his *selling* time is worth $30 an hour. That's *four times as much!*

If this same salesman could find a way to spend just one additional hour each day in face-to-face selling activities, he could logically expect to put an additional $30 *each day* in his own pocket.

TIME VALUE CHART

Based on 2,000 working hours per year
(Fifty 40-hour weeks plus two weeks of vacation)

If you earn:	Every hour is worth:	Every minute is worth:	One hour per day for one year is worth:
$ 8,500	$ 4.25	$ 0.07	$ 1,062.50
10,000	5.00	.08	1,250
12,000	6.00	.10	1,500
15,000	7.50	.125	1,875
20,000	10.00	.17	2,500
25,000	12.50	.21	3,125
50,000	25.00	.42	6,250

Your time is valuable to you.

Now that you've set a dollar value on your own time, let's consider some of the other ways you can gain time in your working day and add dollars to your income.

Finding new hours for the sales day

Do you take time to learn your prospects' work schedules? Do your prospects, for example, reserve the first hour of the day for reading their mail and refuse to see salesmen during that period? Is this prospect's lunch hour usually extended to two o'clock in the afternoon? Does this prospect prefer to have you call on Thursdays instead of Wednesdays? Plan your sales calls to fit the work patterns of different prospects and you'll spend far less time sitting in the outer office. You can use this saved time as selling time in the office of some other available-now prospect.

Do you have more than your share of those won't-keep-their-appointments prospects? You can eliminate many unproductive calls by using the telephone. A 10¢ telephone call is an inexpensive way (and time saving, too) to learn about cancelled appointments ahead of time. It's a rare day that goes exactly as planned. So have an alternate schedule handy and follow it if and when your regular appointment schedule is changed.

Here's another timesaver used by professionals. Cut your presentation down to its essential points. Don't talk too much. Don't stay too long. Anticipate objections and answer them in your presentation before they're raised. Trim yourself down for selling and buying. You're not in the prospect's office to converse or debate, you're there to get that order.

Many professionals prefer to presell by sending letters and information ahead of their sales calls. They let the prospect become familiar with new products in the line by reading product brochures and announcement folders. This practice will sharply reduce the time required to explain new products. If you can presell and pre-inform, you'll be able to see more people and sell more people in a given selling day.

Don't be caught short by cancelled appointments. Know who you will see if extra time becomes available in your day. And while you're cooling your heels in the reception room, have you ever thought of using this time to review your presentation, make out call reports, and study technical information about your own or competitive products?

It's really not difficult to add extra hours to your working day, and you don't have to exert undue pressure on yourself. If you'll review your own personal selling habits you'll be surprised at the time you can save with an organized time usage plan.

Let's refer back to our Mr. Average Salesman and break down his expenditure of nonbusiness hours:

Personal Time Expenditures

Sleeping	7.0 hours
Eating	
Breakfast	.5
Lunch	1.0
Dinner	1.0
Shower and morning dress activities	.5
Working time	8.0
Recreation, relaxation, etc.	5.0
One day of business life	24.0 hours

Compare his time expenditures with yours. Now for the important question. Can you gain 10 minutes here and 15 minutes there to add to your working hours? Professional salesmen do this and that's one of the reasons they're professionals.

WEEKLY TIME ANALYSIS CHART

	Monday	Tuesday	Wednesday	Thursday	Friday	Saturday	Sunday	Total
Planning Time								
Prospecting								
Scheduling								
Miscellaneous								
Pre-call Time								
Traveling								
Waiting								
Other								
Selling Time								
New Prospects								
Old Prospects								
Customers								
Administrative Time								
Processing Orders								
Making Reports								
Other								
Personal Time								
Meals								
Sleep								
Recreation								
Miscellaneous								
Total time recorded								

"Only selling time produces dollars."

Up to this point we've considered those areas where time might be saved for you. But do you know for certain just how you are now spending your time? Are you absolutely sure?

Many professionals I know have a habit of keeping track of their time. They know without question exactly where, when, and how they spend it. If you'll prepare and keep your own time chart (one similar to that shown on page 184) you'll be amazed to learn how much "air" there is in your supposedly tight time schedule.

Keeping track of your own selling day or selling week isn't an easy thing to do. If you feel such a task will be boring, that's good! Successful salesmen, psychologists agree, seldom have an aptitude or even a tolerance for clerical tasks. The very interest pattern which makes you a successful salesman will make you shudder at the thought of keeping track of your time.

But I can guarantee that keeping track of your time will pay handsome dividends. And I'll further guarantee that if you'll keep such a chart for just one week, you'll be astonished at the selling time you've lost and will want to find new ways to save time and use it to become a more successful, happier, and richer salesman.

When habits are young they are like lion cubs, fluffy, funny, frolicsome little animals. They grow day by day. Eventually they rule you.

— Elbert Hubbard

Psycho-Sales-Analysis Guide

After reading Section 12, write
your answers to these questions:

1. How much is one hour of face-to-face selling time worth to me? Use the formula below.

$$\frac{\text{Annual Income}}{\substack{\text{Total hours spent each year} \\ \text{face-to-face with legitimate prospects}}} = \substack{\text{Value of each} \\ \text{selling hour}}$$

2. What would these people say if I asked them where or how they thought I was wasting my time?

    a. My boss.

    b. My wife.

    c. My fellow salesmen.

    d. My prospects and customers.

3. In order of their importance, what are three areas in which I can save time for more productive sales activities?

4. If I properly applied the time savings from question 3, how much additional income could I expect to make? (Use the formula in question 1 to compute your answer.)

5. Specifically what can I do to increase the number of productive sales calls I make each week?

6. If I were an ideal salesman, how would my selling day be spent? Prepare an ideal time schedule.

Section 13

Psycho-Sales-Analysis Guide

*Before reading Section 13, write
your answers to these questions:*

1. What personality traits do I *like* to find in other people?

2. What personality traits do I *dislike* finding in other people?

3. Which of the above personality traits do I possess?

4. What is my most valuable personality trait?

5. What is my least valuable personality trait?

6. What do I consider to be the three most important personality traits for a salesman?

7. If asked to state my best and my worst personality traits, what would these people probably say?

   a. My boss.

   b. My wife.

   c. My best friend.

How to improve
your selling personality

Contrary to all the sales principles you've studied, it isn't absolutely necessary that your prospects be charmed by your personality. One of the most successful insurance salesmen I've ever known has a personality that makes his prospects cringe. One of his clients once said to him:

"Mr. T_____, I'll buy your damned policy if you'll just promise me one thing."

"What's that?" asked Mr. T_____.

"Promise me you'll never come into my office or try to see me again," the prospect told him.

"Agreed," said Mr. T_____ without a moment's hesitation. "Just put your name here on this line."

Now, if you're ready for the big surpise in this true story, Mr. T_____ is a member of his company's Million Dollar Sales Club. He's been a member for the past 10 years.

Please note that I've said it isn't *absolutely* necessary that your prospects like you. Mr. T_____ is successful only because he has drive, perseverance, and knows how to use basic techniques of the selling profession. However, as I'm sure you'll realize, Mr. T_____ is an exception to the rule. Every time he is rude to a prospect he places a hurdle in his own path. Just think of all the additional insurance this man could have sold if he practiced common courtesy and cultivated a pleasing personality.

Most people prefer to buy from salesmen they like. The salesman who is better liked than his competitors certainly has the edge in selling. So we can say that it is highly desirable for salesmen to develop personalities that help, rather than hinder, their selling efforts.

Today's buyer is better educated and more sophisticated than his counterpart of yesterday. Harold Hill, the back-slapping, sharp-tongued, quick-witted salesman of the musical *Music Man,* would probably starve to death as a salesman in today's competitive climate. Today's professional knows that people no longer buy simply because they are gullible and like the salesman. However, today's salesman also understands that if his prospects and customers like him, they will be more apt to trust him, listen to his story, and buy his products.

What makes a successful salesman?

Let's analyze some of the personality traits of successful salesmen. But first, let's recognize that they are not supermen. They put on their pants one leg at a time just as the rest of us do. They have their idiosyncrasies and their faults. They are often lacking in traits which most of us consider commendable. Yet they have many personality traits in common.

Not long ago one of the nation's largest sales and marketing clubs attempted to separate and study the factors which make salesmen "star producers." Their survey included information about the top salesmen in more than 50 large companies and enabled them to develop a personality profile of the successful salesmen in their area. Here's what this survey revealed:

Mental abilities. Successful salesmen are much more intelligent than the average man on the street. The salesmen studied in this survey, the top producers, tested far above average in the use and comprehension of language, numerical and verbal reasoning, and in visual accuracy. These salesmen, in short, had an exceptional ability to think on their feet and to communicate with other people.

Personal interests. Successful salesmen, this survey disclosed, have less than average interest in mechanical and computational subjects. They do not have an interest in clerical functions or in scientific subjects as a rule. They rank average in their artistic, literary, and social service interests.

What are these salesmen interested in? The top producers tested had a keen interest in the art of evoking decision and in getting other people to do things their (the salesman's) way. And not surprisingly, they thoroughly enjoyed the challenge in the game of selling.

Temperament patterns. As might be expected, the successful salesman being tested had more temperamental drive than Mr. Average Citizen. The survey pictures the more successful salesman as a man who is energetic, self-assured, and highly sociable. He is emotionally stable, objective, and agreeable. He is neither impulsive nor restrained, superficial nor reflective, and can be ranked average in these temperament traits. One of his far-higher-than-the-average-man traits is trust in other people. Apparently this trust in others evokes a like feeling among his prospects, and they, in turn, have a high degree of trust in the salesman.

Motivation. What is it that makes a successful salesman go? What psychological factors drive this man forward? According to this survey the star salesman is not concerned with the feelings of his fellow man. His motivation is one of individualism. His driving force, it seems, comes from his desire to dominate others and his keen interest in money.

In summary, this survey describes the more successful salesman as a man with the dominant personality traits of *sales acumen, persuasiveness, desire to dominate,* and *profit-mindedness.*

Now, then, how can *you* go about improving your sales personality? How can you become a more successful man through improved personality?

As an adult your personality is already well developed. It can, however, be reinforced and improved *if* you are willing to look at the separate facets of your personality, drag them out into the open, and take the necessary steps to polish and improve them.

Basic traits form personality

Let's begin by recognizing that certain basic character traits are required for success in any professional field, and selling is no exception. These traits are the raw materials with which our personalities are constructed — the "basic building blocks" of our personalities:

1. *Loyalty.* Few companies will retain salesmen who are disloyal to the organization. Remember, too, that customers who feel a salesman is not loyal to their interests will not continue to do business with him.

2. *Stability.* Who likes to do business with moody people, cry babies, and socially immature individuals? No one does.

3. *Self-Reliance.* As a general rule, salesmen work by themselves with little or no direct supervision. There's seldom anyone around to pick them up and put them back on their feet when the going gets rough. They have to be self-starters and self-restarters. That's how the game is played.

4. *Competitiveness.* Selling is no profession for quitters. The desire and the drive to beat out the competition is a "must" requirement if a salesman wants to succeed. That "killer instinct" has to be present.

5. *Maturity.* Emotional maturity, social maturity, and professional maturity are all necessary for selling success.

6. *Ambition.* Successful salesmen are never at a loss for something to do. They usually know what they want in life and where they want to go. They think big and chart a direct path toward their goals. Spare time is a luxury they seldom enjoy. They're much too busy making personal progress.

7. *Leadership.* It's impossible to have followers unless you yourself are a leader. Getting others to think as you do and moving them to action requires a high degree of leadership. All successful salesmen are, of necessity, leaders.

In addition to these basic raw materials, a successful salesman needs a driving force. In a world where success is usually graded by financial achievement, money is perhaps the most powerful motivator for salesmen. They like money. They work to get money. Yet money alone seldom provides the push it takes to reach the top. There are other powerful psychological motivators at work inside the successful salesman. The most obvious of these are:

1.   The need to achieve.

2.   The need to excel.

3.   The need to acquire.

4.   The need to be recognized.

5.   The need to serve.

Money may be the means of obtaining these other basic needs, but it is often the needs and not the money which act as the primary motivators in pushing salesmen up the ladder of success.

Working with basic character traits and driving forward by psychological motivators, the successful salesman inevitably develops other traits of character which round out his personality. As he gains knowledge of his company and its products, his basic character traits of loyalty and self-reliance help him build *enthusiasm.* Now he believes so strongly in his product that he cannot wait to tell others about its merits. His personal enthusiasm becomes contagious and infects his prospects.

Enthusiasm, in turn, helps to build self-confidence. If you are enthusiastic about your company and its products, you just know that selling these products will be easy. Your self-confidence radiates outward to inspire your prospect's confidence in you and in the product you sell.

If you would build confidence in the mind of a prospect you must have, first of all, the ability to communicate with him. And since communication is a two-way street, you'll have to show consideration for the prospect's needs, his problems, and his time. You'll have to listen to the prospect as well as talk to him. Your personality, shown by what you say and how you act, can either open or close this vital communications channel between yourself and the prospect.

Other traits add to your appeal

The end personality presented to the prospect is the personality of a well-rounded individual plus other personality essentials which add frosting to the cake. Among the most important of these *extra* personality traits you'll find the following:

Appearance. Professional salesmen dress in a dignified manner. Their appearance shows them to be men of accomplishment, good taste, and substance. This does not require the wearing of white tie and tails. But it does mean that you should dress in keeping with the tastes of your prospects.

Sport coats are out when you're calling on large business firms. A neat, well-pressed business suit, a clean shirt, and shined shoes are the dress of the day. And be careful about those loud neckties; they can, in some circles, create a very poor impression.

If you're calling on farmers, don't dress as a "city slicker" would. You'll be out of step and out of luck, too, when it comes to getting that order.

Here's a personal, and very important note. Mouthwash and deodorant are not sissy products. They're used by the most rugged men and the most successful salesmen. Bad breath and body odor are inexcusable.

Health habits. Successful salesmen are temperate in their eating and drinking habits. Bloodshot eyes and morning-after breath are sure ways to kill a sale. So exercise properly, be moderate in the consumption of both food and drink, and stay in good physical condition. A salesman's life is not an easy one, so why should you handicap yourself?

Success in selling requires *total* health. This means emotional and spiritual health as well as physical health. If personal problems have soured your outlook on life and made you an unhappy person, it will be extremely difficult for you to succeed in the sales field.

If you need professional counseling for personal or psychological problems, go and get it. There's no sin in being unhappy, but resignation and failure to do something about being unhappy is a waste of your God-given talents. An old Arabian proverb expresses a thought which is as true today as it was centuries ago when it was first written: "He who has health has hope, and he who has hope has everything."

Good manners. Though some people may think it's trite, that old Golden Rule works wonderfully well for salesmen. Using the right fork at dinner and being courteous at all times are standard practices of the more successful salesmen.

There's nothing old hat about good social manners. When you're polite you prove that you're aware of and attentive to the needs and wants of other people. You also set yourself apart as a man worth knowing, a man who cares about what other people think.

Efficiency. If you look about at the successful salesmen you know, you'll find that each of them is organized. They plan ahead and organize themselves and their working habits. They keep adequate sales records, control the use of their time, and are efficient and aggressive in the pursuit of their sales goals. Professionals are efficient. They're seldom caught short when the prospect voices an objection — and they have answers ready.

Personal characteristics that win sales jobs

What characteristics do sales managers look for when interviewing applicants for sales jobs? Which traits are the most important in the sales manager's eyes? When asked these questions the sales manager of one of America's largest and most respected firms put his list in this order:

1. Quality of character.
2. Personal industry.
3. Natural ability — physical and mental.
4. Courage.
5. Personality.

"Most people are surprised that we've put personality fifth in our rating system," this sales manager said. "Personality is important, but it takes a back seat to the other selection keys we use."

If you'll think about these characteristics, you'll quickly see why they are considered in this numerical order.

1. *Quality of character* is, in essence, that rare combination of loyalty, sincerity, honesty, and straightforwardness that makes a man a valuable addition to any sales team. This is the priceless ingredient known as personal integrity which prompted Elbert Hubbard to write: "If you work for a man, in heaven's name work for him. Speak well of him and stand behind the institution he represents."

2. *Personal industry* is second only to character. The willingness to work, coupled with the ability to work,

generally makes the difference between an average salesman and a star salesman.

The salesman who knows how to work will intuitively understand the need to cultivate new prospects. In doing this he automatically draws larger commission checks while making more money for the company he represents.

The history of American business shows that we lose 5% of our customers every year because of relocation, bankruptcy, going out of business, and death. Personal industry is required to maintain that constant flow of new prospects.

3. *Natural ability.* A good salesman must have innate ability to learn all there is to know about his products. He must be able to talk in terms that people can understand and, with his skillful application of basic sales principles, make them want his product. He must know his prospects more thoroughly than he knows his products for, in the final analysis, it is people and not products that he is selling.

4. *Courage.* This is the ability to keep going in the face of defeat or discouragement. This is the daring to persevere against any and all odds. This is the mark of a man who has the stomach to fight for the order, and get it!

5. *Personality.* Leaving personality until last doesn't mean it is not important. It is. It is one of the five foremost traits which sales managers seek in their salesmen. It is the salesman's personality which opens the office door and the prospect's heart. It is personality which sets the stage on which the interplay of character, personal industry, ability, and courage can climax in the closing of the sale.

Captain Eddie Rickenbacker, World War I ace and board chairman of Eastern Air Lines, describes the successful salesmen he has known in these words:

"He is a man with faith, honesty, belief in the freedom to work; one who is benevolent and charitable, thrifty, and loving of his country, his family, his job and himself. He is a man with mental ability, who is stable and industrious, who will stick with it regardless of the headaches and heartaches, who is loyal, self-reliant, and able to get along with others. He is a leader, who has attained a real degree of maturity, and who has goals which will carry him to the top."*

Here, then, are the basic building blocks which form the foundation for successful sales careers. Review them frequently. Meld them into your own unique personality and work to improve yourself in those areas where you may feel you need improvement. You'll be a far more successful salesman for this effort.

*What a Salesman Should Know About Himself (Chicago: The Dartnell Corp.) Reprinted by permission.

Nine Don'ts Worth Remembering

Don't talk about yourself.

Don't depreciate other people.

Don't gossip.

Don't argue or debate issues with prospects.

Don't lose your composure.

Don't be insincere.

Don't resent constructive criticism.

Don't be negative in your thinking.

Don't violate trusts and confidences.

It's good to have money and the things that money can buy, but it's good, too, to check up once in a while and make sure you haven't lost the things that money can't buy.

— Elbert Hubbard

Psycho-Sales-Analysis Guide

After reading Section 13, write your answers to these questions:

1. What is the order of importance to *me* of the following psychological motivators (rate them 1 through 5):

    a. Need to achieve.

    b. Need to excel.

    c. Need to acquire.

    d. Need to be recognized.

    e. Need to serve.

2. What do I consider to be:

    a. My worst physical health habit?

    b. My worst mental health habit?

3. What steps can I take to become more enthusiastic?

4. How do I rate myself on the following traits?

    a. Loyalty.   e. Maturity.

    b. Stability.   f. Ambition.

    c. Self-reliance.   g. Leadership.

    d. Competitiveness.   h. Initiative.

5. Which of the above personality traits should I attempt to improve first?

Section 14

Psycho-Sales-Analysis Guide

Before reading Section 14, write
your answers to these questions:

1. What was the most embarrassing moment in my sales career?

2. Why did the above situation cause me to be embarrassed?

3. Do I have all the self-confidence I need? If not, why not?

4. How do I rate *(poor, fair,* or *excellent)* in these areas?

    a. Knowledge of my product.

    b. Knowledge of my company.

    c. Knowledge of basic selling techniques.

    d. Awareness of my own strengths and weaknesses.

    e. Sincerity.

    f. Faith in the future.

    g. Positive thinking.

5. When was the last time I lost my composure in a selling situation? Describe what happened.

6. Why did I lose my composure? (Are you sure this is the real reason?)

How to build
your self-confidence

A FEW YEARS ago one of the world's greatest salesmen was laid to rest. His name was Winston Churchill.

Here was a man who was recognized as a genius in many fields. He was a soldier, a statesman, a politician, a writer, and an artist. He was a success at almost everything he attempted to do in life. Yet few people realize that his greatest success of all was as a *salesman.*

Who but a professional salesman could have sold a beaten nation the idea that it should rise from its knees to defeat an enemy with unquestioned arms superiority? Who but a professional salesman could have dominated the foreign policies of other nations, infused his own political philosophies into their governmental systems, and held the respect of friend and foe alike for more than half a century?

What was the secret of Winston Churchill's greatness? What single character trait, more than any other, made him the titan of his time?

No one will question Winston Churchill's courage. He had intelligence. He certainly had abilities of many kinds. He possessed sound judgment. He had many traits which are found in other successful men. But more than anything else, Winston Churchill had *confidence in himself.*

The self-confidence of this man poured out and engulfed everyone around him. The entire free world caught the fire of his personal convictions. His self-confidence contributed to winning the greatest war the world has known.

Few men have the capability within themselves to be a Winston Churchill. Few men will ever be able to possess the degree of self-confidence he had. Yet each of us does possess, to some degree, all the character traits of this great man.

Each of us has some ability. Each of us has a measure of judgment. Each of us possesses some intelligence. And each of us has some degree of self-confidence. If we didn't have a little confidence in ourselves, we'd all stay in bed in the morning and pull the protective covers up over our heads.

The secret to becoming more successful than we are now is to take the abilities and traits of character we already possess, and improve and strengthen them.

We'd all agree that a salesman needs to have self-confidence. I'm sure we also agree that the more self-confidence we have the more successful we'll be. So much for theory. So much for platitudes. It all sounds great. But the important question is, how can *you* become more self-confident?

A plan for greater self-confidence

I'm now going to show you a plan which other salesmen have used very successfully to build more self-confidence. It's a program that will work for you, too, if you'll take the time to study and use it.

First, let's recognize the fact that you are the only person in this world who can do something about your own self-confidence. No one else can do it for you. Becoming more self-confident is strictly a do-it-yourself program. I can tell you how, but the sweat and effort must be yours.

Here are the nine keys which will open the door to a more self-confident you:

1. *Learn all there is to know about your product.* How will knowing more about your product or service help you gain more self-confidence? That's easy. If you knew every conceivable answer about your product you'd never be afraid of any conceivable question a prospect or customer might ask. Right? You'd be an expert in your customer's eyes. You could present a sales story that left no questions unanswered and every product benefit fully explained. You'd never be afraid of being embarrassed. Wouldn't that make you more self-confident? You can bet it would!

This is one of the major reasons why successful salesmen are self-confident. They know their products from A to Z.

Today, while the thought is still fresh in your mind, resolve that you are going to know more about your product than any other salesman in the world.

This is a big decision. It will take a great amount of effort and study. But you can get this knowledge (and the self-confidence that goes along with it) *provided* you're willing to pay the price of extra effort.

2. *Develop a professional attitude toward selling.* Next to your wife, your family, and your health, there's nothing that's more important in your life than selling. This is your livelihood. Being casual about a thing that's this important to you seems absurd, and it is!

Look at the successful salesmen you know. You'll find they are always on time for appointments. They always have well-prepared and well-rehearsed presentations. They are organized in their selling habits. They are well groomed and dressed. They have, in other words, a professional attitude toward selling and, as a result, are better able to do a more professional job.

A thought without a following act is a useless mental exercise. "I'll start tomorrow" just isn't good enough. The professional starts today. He makes up his mind that he is going to be a professional. His attitude — his decision to act — is the necessary starting point. And he always follows through with *action.*

Decide today that you are going to be the expert in your particular sales field. You're going to be *the* top salesman in your sales organization. Anything less will be unacceptable to you. You're going to graduate from the semipro league and join the professional ranks *today.*

If you were recognized by your prospects and customers as a professional salesman, wouldn't that recognition make you more self-confident? Undoubtedly it would. That's why developing a professional selling attitude will give you added self-confidence.

3. *Be positive and decisive.* How can we recognize people who have more than the normal amount of self-confidence? They act positively and decisively, don't they? They make strong statements and leave no doubt that they are ready to support those statements with facts.

Now ask yourself this question: Are these people self-confident because they are positive and decisive, or are these people positive and decisive because they are self-confident? Which came first — the chicken or the egg?

The truth of the matter is that self-confidence and positive, decisive actions are almost one and the same. If you want to become more self-confident, one of the easiest ways to do this is to act more positively and decisively.

There's a bit of the actor in all successful salesmen. They thoroughly enjoy being the center of the stage in selling situations. But it can't be just acting or the curtain will slam down suddenly and often.

If you want to be a self-confident, positive, decisive salesman try these things:

Restudy all the features and benefits of your product or service. Rework your selling approach so that it flows in a logical, organized pattern. Practice, practice, and practice some more. Then you'll find it's easy to act positively and decisively because you know what you're doing is right. Will this make you more self-confident? I guarantee that it will.

While we're on this subject, let's cover another base. We've all had our bad days. The wife feels neglected because we've spent three evenings in a row on sales calls. We've put our job ahead of her and the children. Wives resent such things. So our breakfast is no picnic and we leave the house in a huff. (If you're not single I'm sure you've lived through situations like this.)

Now, professional ballplayers have similar problems. Yet they don't carry their domestic problems out onto the playing field. When they step up to home plate they're not brooding over the spat they had at the breakfast table. They have just one, single thought in mind. That's to drive the baseball over the left field wall. They have a professional attitude. Their mind is locked on the job at hand. They're positive and decisive.

Successful salesmen follow the lead of the sports professional. They put their personal problems aside when they are "up to bat." They concentrate on the job at hand. They have to, or they won't remain in the professional league of salesmanship.

Don't let personal problems cloud your selling day. Work at being positive and decisive. You'll be surprised at how much more self-confidence you'll have using this simple technique.

4. *Analyze your successes and failures.* I play golf for the fun of it. Most of us do. But not the professional golfers. They have to make their living at this game. When they slice a ball, it isn't just another bad shot, it's a shot that could cost them thousands of dollars in prize money. So golf professionals remember what they did wrong. They change

their stance, concentrate on their follow-through, or straighten their elbows. What happens? The next shot is right down the middle of the fairway.

Professional salesmen, like professional golfers, also make a bad shot now and then. If the professional salesman is wise, he'll make sure he knows why he lost the sale.

Do you always know why you failed to get a signature on the order form? Do you know what went wrong on that last sales call? What could you have said or done to change the outcome? Did you make a mistake? What was it? Unless you can answer these questions and identify that particular mistake, this lack of knowledge could cost you the order on your next sales call.

And what about those successful sales calls? When you walk out with a signed order, do you know why this man bought from you? Are you absolutely sure this is the reason? Your next prospect may buy for the very same reason.

Analyze your failures and your successes. Then you'll know both what to do and what not to do on the following sales calls.

Would you be more self-confident if you knew that what you were doing was absolutely correct? Sure you would.

5. *Be sincere at all times.* If you know in your heart that your prospect doesn't really need your product, don't try to sell it to him. Even the worst of us have twinges of conscience when we do something that's contrary to our personal mores and beliefs. These twinges of conscience can quickly tear down any self-confidence we have. Insincerity, no matter how slight, should be avoided like the plague. Peddlers may sneer at the Golden Rule, but professional salesmen lean on it for support.

How can we be sure that the prospect does or does not need our product? We can take the time to observe, question, or research *before* we sell him.

Being honest with ourselves can give us that good feeling which builds up our self-confidence. Old-fashioned thinking? Not a bit! Personal integrity is a necessary requirement for professional salesmen and sincerity is a big part of integrity. Successful salesmen take care of their customers, and their customers, in turn, take care of them.

6.   *Have faith in your prospects.* Have you ever purchased an item from someone you didn't trust? If you did you must have wanted the item he was selling in the worst way. You were willing to take a chance and your buying was an exception to the rule.

Unless your prospect trusts you, the odds are against his buying from you. Trust, you'll find, is a two-way street. So have faith in your prospect's desire to be fair with you and some of that faith will rub off on him.

How will trusting your prospects help you become more self-confident? Wouldn't you feel more at ease in the presence of a trusted friend than in the presence of someone you didn't trust? It's a cruel, hard world, but successful salesmen are always willing to trust a prospect until the prospect's actions prove him untrustworthy. This simple practice puts the salesman at ease and is a very effective builder of self-confidence. It will work for you if you'll use it.

7.   *Act the part of a professional salesman.* You're a knowledgeable, competent salesman, so why hide your light under a bushel basket? Extend yourself a bit. Act the part of the professional. You know a great many things about your product that your prospect doesn't know. So counsel him on these points. Act in a professional manner and your prospect will see you as a professional.

Will acting the professional salesman's role give you added self-confidence? Yes, unquestionably it will. Each time an actor does his part in a play he becomes more polished and more confident. Salesmen while selling and actors while acting have many points of similarity.

8.   *Think positively*. Sometimes when the selling is hard it's difficult to keep a positive attitude. You've had a bunch of no's thrown in your face. You begin to doubt that your product can be sold or that you are capable of selling it. Watch out! You're about to catch *negative-think-itis*.

Stand aside and remember all of those successes you've enjoyed. You were successful before and you can be successful again, if you'll only believe in yourself and your proven ability. Don't let those self-doubts cloud the picture.

It's the ability to pick oneself up off the floor and start again that separates the professional from the amateur salesman. You're not alone. There's never been a salesman who, at one time or another, hasn't had to face a problem just like yours. Others have made a comeback and you can make one, too!

Check yourself occasionally for *negative-think-itis*. When your prospect asks a question do you immediately become defensive? Do you turn his question around in your mind and see it as an objection? Do you prolong your answer with detailed explanations when a simple answer was all that was required? If so, you've begun to exhibit the symptoms of *negative-think-itis*.

Do you pride yourself on your positive attitude? Do you always think positively? Then tell me, what do you call the traffic control device with the red, yellow, and green lights?

Most people refer to these devices as "stop lights." They consider these devices a hindrance. These lights keep them from arriving at the office on time, make them late for appointments, and slow down their driving.

What people are forgetting is that these lights are placed at intersections to *help* drivers. They stop the cross traffic so that you can drive your car safely through an intersection.

These lights are green just as often and as long as they are red. So, why shouldn't we call them "go lights"?

Spend your time thinking of all the reasons why your prospect *should buy* from you. Stop worrying about all the reasons why he *shouldn't buy.* Do this and I can guarantee you'll become a more positive-thinking salesman and have more self-confidence.

9. *Smile.* Smiles are a very effective, non-verbal communication bridge. When you smile at your prospect you're sending a message: "I know what I'm doing. I'm at ease. I'm here to help you. I'm your friend." Your prospect, nine times out of ten, will smile right back at you.

If you doubt the power of a smile try this little experiment: Walk two blocks down a busy sidewalk. In the first block look at people with your face frozen or scowling. Look them directly in the eye. What's their reaction? They'll look away, lower their eyes, frown back, or return your angry expression. Your attitude is reflected in their faces.

Now, in the second block, look each stranger in the eye *and smile.* You'll see the difference immediately. Now these strangers will smile back at you. Their expressions will seem to be saying, "I've probably met this man somewhere before." These people are friendly. And be sure to notice what's happening to you. You'll sense a warm glow inside. In case you don't happen to recognize that glow — *that's your self-confidence beginning to show.*

Make a checklist

As you can see, there's really no secret to becoming more self-confident. The key is to realize that self-confidence must come from within yourself.

Make a checklist of these nine self-confidence building techniques. Keep it handy and refer to it at periodic intervals. By knowing what to do and by practicing you can have that degree of self-confidence you always wanted.

How can I be sure that these techniques will work for you? I've seen them work for hundreds of salesmen just like you. There's no reason why you can't begin today to be a more self-confident (and more successful) salesman.

The habit of self-confidence is a result of the habits of industry and concentration.
— *Elbert Hubbard*

Psycho-Sales-Analysis Guide

*After reading Section 14, write
your answers to these questions:*

1. What specific program can I follow to:

    a. Learn more about my products?

    b. Learn more about my company?

2. What specific program can I follow to:

    a. Learn more about competitive products?

    b. Learn more about competitive companies and their marketing operations?

3. What steps can I take to make my sales presentations more dynamic? More positive? More decisive?

4. Which of the confidence-building techniques mentioned in this section can be the most help to me?

5. How, specifically, can I use the above-mentioned confidence-building techniques?

6. How do I analyze the results of my last six sales calls? (Describe the call, whether it was a success or a failure, and why.)

7. Why does the most successful salesman among my acquaintances have more self-confidence than I do?

Section 15

A master plan
to increase your sales

SOME OF these ideas look good on paper, but will they really work for me? If this question has occurred to you, don't feel you're alone in being a "doubting Thomas." Questions such as this are asked every time a group of salesmen are exposed to new or unfamiliar concepts.

"My territory, my product, my prospects, and my customers are different," insists the salesman, and he's partially right. But what he forgets is that he isn't selling a territory, a product, prospects, or customers — *he is selling people.*

Now, it's true that people are different. But those different people have common needs, common wants, and common desires, and they're motivated by essentially the same psychology. It's these common denominators which enable salesmen to use the same basic selling techniques to sell different products to different people.

Knowing how to sell and selling are two entirely different things. You can read hundreds of books, know and understand all that is written in them, and still fail as a salesman. Knowledge for knowledge's sake is useless. It's the application of knowledge that gets the job done. It's the doing that determines the size of those commission checks.

All right, how can *you* use the information in this book to increase your own sales effectiveness and your income? The answer lies in a planned program which adapts these basic principles and techniques to your own individual selling situation. Who is the only person who can develop such a plan? That person is *you!*

If a sales program is to be successful, it must be well planned and well organized. It should be logical and follow an orderly progression. It should bring the prospect over to your way of thinking, step by step, until he agrees with you that he does have the need, the ability to buy, the desire to buy, and that he should buy, right now.

Organize your sales program

If you think back to your school days, you'll recall that outlines were the key to organizing your reports and themes. First you gathered your information. Then you outlined your theme. The end result was a paper that progressed in an orderly fashion from beginning to end with continuity in the thoughts you wished to express.

This same procedure is used by professional salesmen to organize their personal sales programs. This programmed sales procedure is a well-proven method which you can use to become more successful than you'd have thought possible. Here are the two steps you can now take to build your own personalized, professional selling program:

Step 1. Gather your information and plans. Go back and read this book again. Underline the important points you want to remember. Pay special attention to the answers you gave to the Psycho-Sales-Analysis Guide questions. Revise them if you wish.

This is the basic information you'll need. These are the building blocks of your own personalized "success plan."

Step 2. Outline your sales future. Now you're ready to start to work on your own "sales success" outline. This is your guide to improved sales performance and greater income. Begin with the first step on The Golden Stairway to Successful Sales: finding better prospects.

List the places where you'll look for those better prospects. List the qualifying factors that make them legitimate prospects for the products or service you sell. Write it all down — who, what, when, where, why, and how.

Work through each of the sales steps and you'll have a startling new view of your personal sales program. Now you'll have an organized plan of battle for that sales dollar, a plan that's built on proven sales techniques and practices. Your thoughts are becoming organized; so is your sales plan.

By this time you've learned which areas of your personal sales program need the most attention and improvement. Now only one item is missing: your *personal goal.*

What do you want to achieve in life? Your first thought will probably be "money." That's the easy and obvious answer. But you want other things a successful sales career can provide.

Perhaps you want to become an executive in your company. What kind of executive? What timetable do you want to set for reaching this goal? You may aspire to early retirement. At what age? Be specific and detailed when you set these personal goals.

Don't sell yourself short

Don't fall into the trap of selling yourself short. Fear of failure has prevented many a man from reaching out for the full measure of success he's capable of attaining. Certainly, you should be practical. But be objective, too. Don't shoot for small goals. If you find that your goals can be easily achieved, you probably haven't set your sights high enough.

Take the time it requires to put these personal goals in writing. Then they'll become firm objectives rather than vague and indefinite hopes for the future. Written goals are also helpful when those moments of discouragement appear on the scene. Just go back and review those written goals and let them help you renew your determination and enthusiasm.

All large corporations and successful businesses make detailed plans for their future. Production quotas, sales goals, and plant improvement schedules are all fitted into the company's master plan for progress. It's only by planning ahead for the future that private business is able to stay competitive and alive in our free enterprise society.

You're also a member of a free enterprise society. To *you* the most important business in the world is *your* sales program. So why not follow the lead of other successful businesses and *plan your future?*

A sample outline

You've already gathered the necessary building blocks by answering the many questions in this book. Now you're ready to proceed with your plan. The form is not important, but the content and organization are. Here's how Jack Jones might outline his sales future (your plan might be similar).

Jack Jones
January 1, 1971

Career Objectives
To increase my income from a present $12,000 per year to $18,000 per year on or before December 31, 1972. I plan to become a Division Sales Manager for my company by June 1, 1971 and Regional Sales Manager by June 1, 1973. When my income reaches the $15,000 level I will join the Country Acres Club.

Method of Achievement
In order to reach these objectives I must increase my sales by 40% the first year, 65% the second year and 100% the

third year. This will require a complete reorganization of my present selling methods. Here's how I plan to upgrade my sales program:

Prospecting
1.   I will visit the public library each Monday night for the next three weeks to study directories, magazines, and newspapers and to search for new prospects and sales ideas. I will then continue to prospect at the library on the first and third Mondays of each month.
2.   I will make notes on these prospects and qualify them in writing as to their probable needs and ability to buy my products.
3.   I will go through my present prospect files and cull the deadwood on the first of each month. I will plan sales calls on those prospects retained in my file.
4.   Each Saturday morning I will review my list of active customers and select six to be telephoned the following week. I will make these telephone calls between my regular appointments and ask these customers for sales leads. My other Saturday activities will include: (1) planning the next week's itinerary; (2) updating my sales records; (3) completing required reports.

Contacting
1. I am now averaging 8 sales calls per day. I will try to increase the number of my sales calls to 10 per day.
Note: Jack Jones would continue his personal selling program by outlining his intended activities in each of the sales steps on The Golden Stairway to Sales Success.

You'll note that the above sample outline is specific and detailed. The amount of detail you'll need in your plan depends on your own objectives. The key to a good program is not length, it is logical content and organization.

Since this is your own personal plan, it need not be shown to anyone else. But refer back to your plan at regular intervals. Work with it as your guide to the future. Follow it and you'll be an organized salesman.

Review your plan periodically

There's an excellent possibility that you'll want to revise your plan from time to time. Feel free to do this. Situations do change. You will also change in your thinking. Your success plan is a working plan. Don't write it out and forget it. It's much too important a part of your sales career.

You now know the methods which professional salesmen use to plan and organize their future. Now your problem becomes one of putting the information you've gained to practical use. If you'll use these selling basics in your own sales program, and retain a professional attitude toward selling, success can and will be yours.

The future belongs to those who prepare for it, and there's no better time to start your success program than *today!*

Life consists of molting our illusions. We form creeds today only to throw them away tomorrow. The eagle molts a feather because he is growing a better one.

— Elbert Hubbard

Appendix

Appendix

NEED shown by: _____

ABILITY shown by: _____

DESIRE shown by: _____

Name _____

Address _____

_____

_____

Telephone: Office _____

Home _____

Call Date	REMARKS	Date For Follow-up

Prospect Card (1)

This format is for a standard 6 in. by 9 in. card available at any stationery store. The advantage of this larger-than-usual card is that it allows ample space to write down information for follow-up calls. Note that each prospect is qualified as to his need, ability to buy, and desire to buy.

| Name _____ | Tel: _____ |
| Address _____ |
| _____ |

Date	Remarks

Prospect Card (2)

Some salesmen prefer to use 3 in. by 5 in. cards for their records. While these smaller cards do not have a large amount of space for recording information, they are easy to carry and fit handily into a small desk file.

Type Buildings Constructed					
Company Name			Contact		
Address:			Home Address:		
Tel:	Home	Bus.	Source		Date
Call No.	Date		REMARKS		

Prospect Card (3)

This prospect card, designed and used by a building-materials salesman, is an unusual 4-1/2 in. by 8-1/2 in. size. There's ample space, however, for the information this salesman requires.

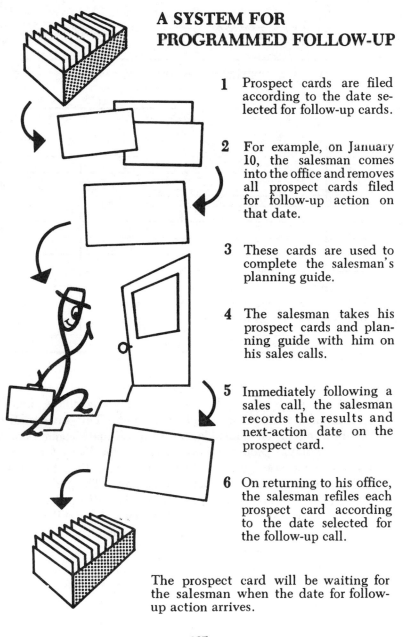

A SYSTEM FOR
PROGRAMMED FOLLOW-UP

1 Prospect cards are filed according to the date selected for follow-up cards.

2 For example, on January 10, the salesman comes into the office and removes all prospect cards filed for follow-up action on that date.

3 These cards are used to complete the salesman's planning guide.

4 The salesman takes his prospect cards and planning guide with him on his sales calls.

5 Immediately following a sales call, the salesman records the results and next-action date on the prospect card.

6 On returning to his office, the salesman refiles each prospect card according to the date selected for the follow-up call.

The prospect card will be waiting for the salesman when the date for follow-up action arrives.

DAILY SALES CALL PLANNING GUIDE

Salesman's name   Date

Call No.	Time	Appt.	Cold Call	Company & Address	Call Objective
	TOTAL:	An extra call a day brings money your way			

Planning Guide

Planning the day's sales calls early in the morning or the night before enables a salesman to plan his route. This saves time while insuring an adequate day and an adequate commission check. Note that a specific call objective is to be listed for each sales call. Some examples are: to introduce your line, to sell a specific product, and to reopen an account. The old adage, "Plan your work and work your plan" is still good advice. This format works equally well as a daily sales-call report. When used for this purpose, the form is completed at the end of the day instead of at the beginning.

DAILY ACTIVITY REPORT

Salesman ——————
Date ——————

Time	Customer & Address	Person Contacted	First call	Follow-up	Telephone	In-Person	Demonstration	Proposal	Next Call Date	COMMENTS

Daily Activity Report

Proper organization and planning of each day's work is a habit of successful salesmen. Many highly successful salesmen use Saturday mornings to plan their weekly schedules with forms like the one above. Use one page for each day.

229

Index